The Fragmentation of Palestine

The Fragmentation of Palestine

*Identity and Isolation since
the Second Intifada*

Joshua Rickard

I.B.TAURIS
LONDON • NEW YORK • OXFORD • NEW DELHI • SYDNEY

I.B. TAURIS
Bloomsbury Publishing Plc
50 Bedford Square, London, WC1B 3DP, UK
1385 Broadway, New York, NY 10018, USA
29 Earlsfort Terrace, Dublin 2, Ireland

BLOOMSBURY, I.B. TAURIS and the I.B. Tauris logo are trademarks of Bloomsbury
Publishing Plc

First published in Great Britain 2022
This paperback edition published 2023

Copyright © Joshua Rickard, 2022

Joshua Rickard has asserted his right under the Copyright,
Designs and Patents Act, 1988, to be identified as Author of this work.

For legal purposes the Acknowledgements on p. xiii constitute an
extension of this copyright page.

Series design by Adriana Brioso
Cover image: Local women gathering produce in Assira Ash-Shamaleyya, 2010.
Courtesy of Joshua Rickard.

All rights reserved. No part of this publication may be reproduced or transmitted
in any form or by any means, electronic or mechanical, including photocopying,
recording, or any information storage or retrieval system, without prior permission
in writing from the publishers.

Bloomsbury Publishing Plc does not have any control over, or responsibility for,
any third-party websites referred to or in this book. All internet addresses given
in this book were correct at the time of going to press. The author and publisher
regret any inconvenience caused if addresses have changed or sites have
ceased to exist, but can accept no responsibility for any such changes.

A catalogue record for this book is available from the British Library.

A catalog record for this book is available from the Library of Congress.

ISBN:	HB:	978-1-7845-3587-2
	PB:	978-0-7556-4653-1
	ePDF:	978-0-7556-4552-7
	eBook:	978-0-7556-4553-4

Typeset by Integra Software Services Pvt. Ltd.

To find out more about our authors and books visit www.bloomsbury.com
and sign up for our newsletters.

This book is dedicated to all the people of Nablus.

Contents

List of Figures		viii
Preface		ix
Acknowledgements		xiii
1	Fragmentation and isolation in Nablus	1
2	Geographical fragmentation	17
3	Political fragmentation	31
4	Social fragmentation	55
5	Development, divisions and debt	73
6	From agricultural resilience to food insecurity	91
7	Storytelling and making sense of the everyday	103
8	Negotiating space and imagery in disoriented landscapes	119
9	Conclusion	131
Notes		141
Index		159

List of Figures

1	Nablus cityscape with Mt. Ebal in the background	15
2	Al-Nasr mosque in the Old City of Nablus	53
3	Palestinian civil defence volunteers	71
4	Local women in the village Assira Ash-Shamaleyya	90
5	Airplane to nowhere	117

Preface

I first visited Nablus in 2007 just after the second intifada but in a period in which the city was still almost totally sealed off from its neighbouring villages and the rest of the West Bank. During this time I worked in the Old City of Nablus as well as Balata refugee camp and the village Awarta. While situated among many other communities in a relatively small geographical region, huge differences existed between these and other Palestinian societies in Nablus. It became clear that while certain class, economic and local differences did exist, these communities had at one time been far more integrated with each other than they presently were, and that many of the drastic differences between them, which were most visible and apparent in the youth, had developed fairly recently. In Awarta and similar villages, it was apparent that the majority of residents had not left the village in several years, whereas in the Old City and to some extent the refugee camps, residents were able to move with limited mobility (excluding during curfews and invasions) within Nablus city, though they rarely did and did not seem to identify with other communities in the area. Despite the severe restrictions on mobility, I was impressed with the levels of cooperation that I witnessed between different residents and the strong sense of community that existed within different areas. Each area seemed to have developed its own modes of social organization for getting by despite the adverse conditions, and residents in each community expressed a sense of identity different than in others.

I returned to Nablus in 2009 to conduct fieldwork for my doctoral research, and was taken aback by the profound changes that had occurred in just two years. Most apparent, that certain restrictions on movement between communities in the area had been eased, and what seemed to be some degree of modernity returning to the devastated city. After long conversations with old friends, I soon realized that while the changes that were taking place seemed positive, they were in fact also having negative impacts on the communities surrounding Nablus. Urban residents of Nablus seemed to have more money than before, but unemployment was high and the majority of them did not have jobs. There were new levels of economic activity in the city centre but rural communities were more deeply impoverished than before and food insecurity was of growing concern. Communities in and around Nablus had been physically isolated from one another throughout the second intifada. The results of isolation have produced profound changes in the ways that these communities function and imagine themselves. This book explores the effects of those changes on the communities and how the people living in them view themselves and their societies. Over time this research has since been expanded to trace the social changes which have created further divisions within communities over the following decade until 2020. In examining social change and modernity, this also raises questions in regard to the paradox of existing in the absence of certainty and citizenship in an area under siege and occupation, while also being brought into an increasingly globalized society by neoliberal capitalism. The names of individuals and certain locations have been changed in order to protect their identities.

Nablus as a city and community has a long and complicated history with surrounding communities and an often contentious relationship with foreign occupying powers. The city's unique situation in the early twenty-first century of having endured eight years of intense military siege, during which official institutions collapsed and in-fighting between rival gangs and political factions through the city into chaos and uncertainty, and then suddenly being exposed to external development projects, made Nablus an ideal case study for understanding the process of social fragmentation that Palestinians were living with. I also choose to concentrate on the Nablus region because of the drastically different realities that existed within a very limited geographic area.

Jabal an-Nar, or *Mountains of Fire*, refers to the reputation of the population of Nablus as a stubborn and fierce people in violent dispute with external authority.[1] The name was ascribed to the city in the early nineteenth century when the people of Nablus repealed the invasion on Napoleon's army by setting fire to the forest of the mountains surrounding Nablus burning the advancing soldiers.[2] Nablus further entrenched this reputation in uprisings against Ali Pasha of Egypt, the British and Jordanian rule.[3] During the second intifada the city resisted through multiple Israeli invasions and became inhospitable to the extent that even the Palestinian Authority could not operate. This city, rich in history and narratives, also situates the experience of Nablus against a unique and colourful backdrop.

This book is intended to illustrate the systematic social fragmentation of Palestinian society. By looking at communities that have experienced long-term isolation imposed by military siege, and the social and political realities that have developed as a result, this illustrates the systematic division of Palestinian communities and the subsequent dissolving of social cohesion. In examining such issues, I focus on not only logistical matters such as how the community survives in adverse situations, but also how 'severed' communities imagine themselves and their futures with reference to a Palestinian discourse which used to link the entirety of the nation and has since become extremely contained and disparate.

Varying levels of imposed isolation have had an assortment of effects on different Palestinian communities. Throughout different periods of time, issues of isolation have forced communities to develop new social networks as well as adapt pre-existing ones in order to allow the community to continue to function despite strict restrictions on the movement of people, products and information. While some communities have been able to compensate for the lack of infrastructure and civil institutions that resulted from siege and the absence of a legitimate indigenous government, others have failed. Many rural villages in the West Bank, which during the most difficult years of the second intifada had been resilient in enduring the hardships of occupation, have in recent years been unable to maintain social cohesion and become fragmented. Isolation has been brought about by military checkpoints and sieges of villages, and since as a result different communities have been divided from one another over long spans of time, new social divisions between communities have developed. Political and social divisions have also developed within communities as a result of internal disputes between political actors, as well as through the surveillance activities of a variety of entities competing for power and control. More relevant to my argument than how the conditions of isolation have occurred is what this isolation means to communities that are severed from those surrounding them.

The book explores fundamental questions with regard to immobility and what it means to remain static. Observing the Palestinian village under siege as an isolated world, we can ask how are individual and community identities formed in the context of a society confined within tight boundaries? What are the effects of these boundaries on the community in spatial, temporal, political and social terms? When someone spends their life in a world confined by siege, what is the impact on their sense of self and community? To what extent does an individual's awareness of surrounding communities and their glimpse into the outside world through technology affect their sense of place in the world? What does it mean to linger stagnant in the world?

Acknowledgements

I am grateful to the editors at I.B. Tauris who have kept this book on track and to the reviewers for their detailed and insightful comments. This monograph was made possible by a research fellowship at the Middle East Institute at the National University of Singapore. I am indebted to my colleagues who looked over and supported this work especially Ali Kadri who provided constant encouragement and ideological inspiration. In the early stages of my research I am thankful to have received the guidance of Toby Kelly, Michael Fischer and Glenn Bowman. I am grateful to Mio Saito who has given me encouragement and support to finish this project. In Japan I was encouraged by long discussions with colleagues especially Shin Takahashi and Kaz Kedia and support from my friends and comrades Iyas Salim and Hirochi Tanaka. Yoshimi Osawa provided me with consultation without which this would not have been possible.

Most of all I am grateful to those who helped me in the field who are too many to name. Over many years I have been grateful for the friendships and long conversations with Saed Abu-Hijleh and Hakim Sabbah who provided me with open doors and social foundations in Nablus. Maroof Rabba' has repeatedly welcomed me in Nablus and provided me with deep insights into the community. Hiba Yousef, Mohammad Samara and many others helped me at various times in gathering local information. I owe a particular debt of gratitude to Qossay Abu Zaitoun who has helped me with my research as well as life both in and outside of Nablus over many years.

1

Fragmentation and isolation in Nablus

Burin is a small village in the northern West Bank, which is particularly well known for its fig cultivation. Every year during the harvest session the residents of the village bring their figs to sell in the markets of Nablus and other nearby villages, where they will also purchase vegetables and other products. Rashid, with whom I was sipping tea, had been appointed mayor of the small village, a symbolic title more than anything since he, like all of the other residents of this small community, sustains his family through agriculture. One year, as the harvest session drew to a close, the residents noticed that the Israeli military had erected new checkpoints on the roads leading out of the village, and would not allow any of the residents to pass. Being unable to move their figs to market, the villagers took their produce over the mountains at night, using tractors. In the following days the Israeli military confiscated all of the tractors in the village. Afterwards, the villagers resorted to bringing their figs over the mountains to market on donkeys, but it was not long before the military entered the village and confiscated all of the donkeys. When I asked Rashid how the village coped after that, he simply replied: 'We ate a lot of figs that year.'

This story, like countless others that I heard while conducting fieldwork in Palestine, demonstrates a sense of antagonism and imposed control over life by the Israeli authorities that is felt on some level or another by all Palestinians living in the occupied territories. The example also illustrates the type of imposed isolation that many Palestinian communities have struggled with, particularly during the years of the second intifada (2000–5). Varying levels of isolation have had an assortment of effects on different Palestinian communities. On some levels, throughout different periods of time, issues of isolation have forced communities to develop new social networks as well as adapt pre-existing ones in order to allow the community to continue to function despite strict restrictions on the movement of people, products and information. While some communities have been able to compensate for the lack of infrastructure and civil institutions that resulted from siege and the absence of an indigenous government, others have failed. Many rural villages in the Nablus area that, during the most difficult years of the second intifada, had been resilient in enduring the hardships of occupation have in recent years been unable to maintain social cohesion and become fragmented. Isolation has been brought about by military checkpoints and sieges of villages, and since as a result different communities have been divided from one another over long spans of time, new social divisions between communities have developed. Political and social divisions have also developed within communities as a result of internal disputes between political actors as well as through the surveillance activities of a variety of entities competing for power and control. More relevant to my argument than how the conditions of isolation have occurred is what this isolation means to communities that are severed from those surrounding them.

Overview

This book takes a critical look at the ways in which cohesion and collective identity have developed and changed in communities in the Nablus region of the West Bank which, since the second intifada, have become isolated from one another in a variety of ways. The ever-changing situation of occupation, political instability and everyday life in Palestine has had profound effects on the ways in which communities have, and have not, functioned in order to compensate for disrupted infrastructure and maintain social cohesion among their populations. After the signing of the Oslo Accords in 1993 and 1995, and increasingly after the second intifada, West Bank communities have become progressively more physically isolated from one another due to military and settler activity. In more recent years, social and political divisions within the larger Palestinian community itself have left many areas socially isolated from one another. These issues of isolation have resulted in the deterioration of infrastructure, civil institutions and social stability in West Bank communities. The aims of this book are to examine how communities in situations of severe isolation work to create structures and networks to compensate for the lack of social maintenance and stability, and how community-based forms of collective identity develop around this. Through examining the literature on the current and historical situations of the Palestinian people and tracing the life histories and experiences of individuals living in communities that have become divided from one another, this book demonstrates changes in community structure and power relations that have taken place in Nablus area communities from the second intifada in 2000–5, and beyond. Nablus remained under military siege for eight years into 2008, during which time neighbourhoods and villages were geographically divided from one another and frequently under harsh curfews, at the time the Palestinian Authority (PA) had little presence or control in the city. Following 2009 and 2010 various levels of limited freedom of movement were restored but within strict confines and other changes in class and lifestyles between different communities led to new challenges. This research traces the social changes that occurred, and divisions which became normalized among the West Bank population, from the second intifada until 2020. This pivotal time span has seen the most severe forms of military-imposed isolation on Palestinian communities as well as the deterioration of the micro-social structures that have held these communities together.

There are two types of isolation being explored: The first is the physical fragmentation of the West Bank due to the Israeli occupation that has greatly restricted the movement of people, products and information from one community to another over extended periods of time. The second type of isolation being looked at is the internal isolation between Palestinian communities that have resulted from political and social fragmentation. Increasingly divisions have grown within rural and urban Palestinian communities. Marginalized communities in Nablus such as rural villages and refugee camps have experienced greater forms of isolation due to power struggles between political factions and various external interests, which have left these areas relatively alienated by the Palestinian Authority and the Palestinian elite. This book examines how communities compensate for the lack of functioning infrastructure and severed social networks, and will explore how community identity is maintained and perceived.

As refugees, minorities and occupied people with an ambiguous citizenship status, the majority of Palestinians, regardless of where they live, face varying complex levels of surveillance.[1] Issues of population surveillance in the West Bank and Gaza have become increasingly complicated with the establishment of the PA. Colonialism, state construction and sovereignty involve multiple levels of surveillance, including establishing and controlling borders, population registration and the distribution of identity cards.[2] Movement through space within and surrounding the Palestinian territories involves encountering various political and surveillance apparatuses, which can have different and changing meanings in different contexts. Shifts in the policies of the Israeli military, the PA and international organizations that operate inside of the occupied territories, and the relationships of these various entities with one another create complex issues of daily uncertainty that may dramatically affect an individual's ability to anticipate their imminent future. Frequent changes in the labels pertaining to autonomy over space and the citizenship status of individuals mean that the life experiences of Palestinians vary dramatically depending on their location – for example, the status of Palestinians who hold Jerusalem identity cards in comparison with those in the West Bank and Gaza who do not. The PA, as an institution responsible for record keeping and the implementation of Palestinian identity cards and passports, has made Palestinian identity in the form of 'citizenship' something tangible. Without a formal government, Palestinians lacked citizenship after 1948, after which those residing in the West Bank and Gaza became Jordanian or Egyptian subjects. After the occupation in 1967, the citizenship status of Palestinians was changed depending on the area in which they were residing. Following the creation of the Palestinian Authority in 1995, the status of some Palestinians was again changed, while others, depending on their situation, maintained varying levels of statelessness. Through defining and regularly redefining the status of individuals and spaces, and through notions of citizenship, jurisdiction and borders, the Palestinian experience is made up of constantly changing legal, political and economic circumstances.[3] In the same way the PA and what it has come to symbolize for Palestinians can be drastically different depending on the period of time, community, political affiliation or economic situations of the individuals defining it.

By looking at the historical situations of Palestinian communities and the development of a nationalist consciousness that is uniquely Palestinian as it has evolved into the contemporary situation of division and limbo, this book aims to address how a collective Palestinian identity has dissolved into community-based forms of identity in a context of isolation and internal conflict. In answering this question I focus on not only logistical matters such as how the community survives and functions as an organic unit in adverse situations, but also how 'severed' communities imagine themselves and their futures with reference to a Palestinian discourse that used to link the entirety of the nation and now has become extremely contained and disparate.

Formations of identity

Palestinian political identity has frequently been viewed as a recent phenomenon and response to the collective antagonism and denial of Zionism and the Nakba.[4] While it is true that narrative surrounding dispossession, exclusion and becoming an 'Other' by those who view themselves distinctly different is dependent on the Israeli counterpart,[5] the formation of a Palestinian political identity can be observed since at least the 1880s.[6] During the late Ottoman and Mandate periods, new middle-class formations in Palestine and Lebanon grew due to connections through protestant missionaries and opportunities in international education, particularly in Christian communities.[7] A growing middle class and intelligentsia during the early twentieth century spawned a demand for Arabic newspapers to share international affairs and, in particular, the activities of the British empire. In 1914, Najib Nassar, journalist and owner of the Haifa-based newspaper *Al-Karmel*, called on Arabs to show support for the Palestinians as a distinct political community.[8]

Rashid Khalidi has suggested that the centrality of Jerusalem in the minds of residents was a distinctive symbol of national identity among Palestinians during the eighteenth century, not only because of the religious and historical importance to Muslim, Christian and Jewish communities, but also as a cultural centre of the nation which became a popular symbol throughout Palestine.[9] Beshara Doumani, however, argues that in observing Ottoman-era identity formations, it was Nablus, not Jerusalem, which played a central role in regional economic relations and was the main commercial centre.[10] *Jabal Nablus* produced surpluses of olive oil, soap and wheat which not only integrated the city and its periphery with international trade but also exposed the region to various cultural influences at a critical and formative point in history.

In the context of a modern Palestinian national consciousness the antagonism of disposition, non-recognition and settler-colonialism provided the foundations for notions of a collective identity.[11] The destruction of Palestinian population centres and disruption of local formations contributed to the perception of a nation denied and a history interrupted, but also gave way to a new shared narrative of the refugee experience.[12] All conceptions of community are imaginary constructions to the extent that the community exists through the notion of its members conceiving themselves as a group.[13] The conception of what the Palestinian community 'should be' denied articulates the external antagonism as a threat to the collective being of the group and constitutes a component of the wider collective identity.[14] The collective consciousness that emerged gained cohesion through a common social history, shared symbols and demonstrations of struggle and resistance. The isolation imposed during the second intifada in the occupied territories that has fragmented communities by separating them from one another over long periods of time, and the subsequent internal division of the Palestinian community both politically and socially, have resulted in a dissolving of the collective national consciousness and caused the personal identities of Palestinians to become more localized and divided.[15]

Violence, trauma and resistance are central themes in what has developed into a collective Palestinian identity. Identity refers to a sense of group belongingness that is often based around ethnic, religious, political and local affiliations and circumstances, but it is also much more than that. Identity is too often dismissed in anthropological discourse as simply being a process by which individuals relate to one another in a homogeneous community[16] but, when discussed in the sense of Palestinian nationalism, identity is far more dynamic and complex. Palestinian identity involves a sense of living through repeated antagonisms that are felt on an individual level through constant reproductions of social memory drawing reference to the idea of an imagined and ideal 'Palestine'. The antagonism that, as Bowman argues,[17] forged a collective Palestinian identity was emphasized by the Nakba in 1948 when more than 750,000 Palestinians of varying classes, tribes and religions were expelled from what became Israel. The stigma that has developed against Palestinians as a result of the refugee crisis and the repeated antagonisms by Israeli and other forces against Palestinians both in the territories and in diaspora has largely contributed to an affirmation of group identity for the population as an ethnic group regardless of where they settled. As Feldman points out, 'violence is formative; it shapes people's perceptions of who they are and what they are fighting for across space and time – a continual dynamic that forges as well as affects identities.'[18]

Tamari describes a city–village dichotomy[19] in the consciences of early-twentieth-century Palestinians. In the case of Nablus, landowning merchant families living in the city controlled the peasant populations of the surrounding villages in an almost feudal manner, making the relationship one with a degree of contention. Graham-Brown notes the conservative character of Nablus, remarking that, through notable positions such as the municipal council as well as kinship relations, the traditional merchant families still rule Nablus with a particularly conservative tone.[20] The relationship between urban and rural populations shifted to some degree as the Israeli labour market in the 1970s and 1980s absorbed workers from villages as well as the cities.[21] Political mobilization ultimately leading to the first intifada created a sense of solidarity between the different strata in Palestinian society. Since the second intifada and the implementation of various degrees of long-term isolation of different communities, social divisions have dramatically increased between communities in Nablus, and particularly between the urban and rural populations.

Tamari has described at length the creation of two distinct class-based identities among the Palestinian population during the late Ottoman and British mandate periods.[22] These diverse cultures were divided into the cosmopolitan coastal communities and the rural peasant communities residing inland.[23] This divide was, in part, the result of growing European influence in the coastal cities leading to a growth in trade, industry, art and overall wealth, whereas the mainly rural peasant areas continued to subsist on farming and grew indebted to the wealthy land owners who resided in the urban areas, as well as the coast. This also represents one of the first instances of the emergence of class consciousness in an Arab society, for which identity was largely tied to family and *hamula* (clan) affiliation. During the war of 1948, the majority of Palestinians living in coastal cities were made refugees and fled inland and to neighbouring countries. In some instances the now refugee population was able to integrate with existing peasant or urban communities, but in most cases they were confined to refugee camps and developed an entirely new basis for identity.

The cultural and class divide between the two distinctively populations – the coastal cosmopolitan populace and the peasants of the mountains – can be compared to the split that was created more recently between rural and urban West Bank communities during the second intifada. Major social differences between the coastal and inland Palestinians in Tamari's comparison were not so much the result of differences in occupation, for instance, fishing versus agriculture, but of exposure to external, particularly European, influences that the Palestinians residing mountains did not receive. The destruction of the cosmopolitan coastal cities in 1948 caused much of their populations to flee inland to the mountains, where social structure continued to be governed by clan and kinship networks such as *hamula*, *'a'ila* and *'ashira*.[24] After the expulsion from the coast, refugee Palestinians who resettled in the West Bank as well as those in diaspora and those who remained in their previous communities were forced to reformulate their notions of social identity as a common people. A result of the contemporary imposed isolation on West Bank cities and villages and the experience of being confined to one's community has been that people who have spent their childhood or youth during this period have had a completely different experience of life, depending on whether they lived in a rural or urban area. This can be illustrated in many aspects such as relationships and influence of the PA in rural versus urban communities, availability of services and existence of infrastructure (as limited as they may be) and the severity and impact of siege on everyday life. Rural areas have also become increasingly impoverished since the signing of the Oslo Accords and particularly since the end of the second intifada. In this respect not only have the two populations had drastically different experiences of everyday life but there are also limits to how they relate to and identify with one another, which has resulted in the development of social stigma between the two groups and a disruption in nationalist cohesion.

Understanding isolation

Settlement construction, military restrictions and the daily antagonisms that came with the Israeli occupation transformed the West Bank, dividing the landscape both physically and socially and leaving small communities isolated from one another. The confiscation of land to build Israeli-only settlements that quickly turned into cities, and networks of Israeli-only roads that connected them, divided the West Bank, as did the restrictions on water resources and the economic systems inside of Palestinian communities.[25] Many rural communities in the West Bank have had dramatic increases in population but have not been allowed to expand geographically or utilize their resources in order to properly maintain their populations, thus imposing new levels of poverty. A so-called improvement strategy first implemented in the early 1970s by the Israeli military was put in place to freeze the agricultural resources of Arab farmers, including water for irrigating land.[26] Water has instead been rerouted to settlements at an increasing rate since the end of the second intifada. This control over resources has halted agricultural production in many Arab villages and caused dramatic shifts in rural life. Other economic hostilities implemented by isolation, such as strategically positioning checkpoints around agricultural producing villages during the harvest season so that it is not possible for farmers to take their produce to market, have also had devastating impacts on small economies throughout the West Bank.

Historically in the Nablus region, the city was closely tied to its hinterland. While a certain peasant and landlord dichotomy existed, the relations between the city and the villages surrounding it were active and mutually beneficial to those who resided in both the villages and the city.[27] Nablus was the centre for manufacturing and export but also the market on which the surrounding villages relied. Throughout the history of the Ottoman Empire, and well before through the Roman era, Nablus was renowned as a productive capital for the manufacturing of soap, agricultural goods and crafts; Nablus was historically the commercial capital of Palestine. Following the division of the villages from the city and the subsequent isolation of communities imposed during the second intifada, Nablus and its hinterland faced a division that the communities in the region had never before experienced. Different realities can exist in different communities depending on their situations and the daily lives of the people living there. Different social imaginations are 'the ways in which people imagine their social existence' and what 'enables us to carry out the collective practices that make up our social life'.[28] Appadurai's concept of 'imagined worlds'[29] refers to the imaginations that people construct due to the influence of mass media. This concept explores changes in a globalized world, through which the media have connected many individual local worlds. Likewise, the collective identities of existing communities can be either reinforced or diminished as a result of migration.[30] In the case of Palestinian communities that have been subjected to long-term isolation from one another, the communities themselves are static worlds of their own in the midst of a larger globalized world in which they exist but from which they are at the same time cut off. The denial of movement to individuals living in Palestinian villages and neighbourhoods that have been effectively severed from one another has led to the physical and social deterioration of the communities in terms of infrastructure, social cohesion and micro-political systems. In addition to the geographical isolation imposed by Israeli colonialism, Palestinian communities have created different identities for themselves which have, over recent years, become dramatically more unique and individual to the specific community. This deterioration in Palestinian identity as a collective nationalist consciousness has developed through layers of geographic, political and social isolation between Palestinian communities, leading to the situation of fragmentation that exists today. This book aims to examine and explain these varying levels of fragmentation using the concept of isolation. As different individuals and communities in Palestine experience life and isolation in different ways, the different communities create different life-worlds according to their circumstances.

Various worlds in the Nablus region

This book is based on ethnographic fieldwork carried out between 2007 and 2020, which relied on participant observation and stories collected in several villages surrounding Nablus as well as the city itself. In order to build an understanding of how different communities have and have not functioned throughout the second intifada, and the ways in which different types of fragmentation have manifested, the communities outside of the city that I have focused on, with the exception of Assira Ash-Shamaleyya,[31] are a series of rural villages to the south and southeast of Nablus. These villages south of Nablus and extending east into the Jordan Valley have historically been important centres of trade and production for Nablus's soap and textile industries. Olive oil, limestone and vegetables were primarily produced in these villages until the occupation of the West Bank in 1967, after which the vast majority of labourable men left to work in Israel until the first intifada. Due to the presence of settlements and the restrictions of the second intifada, these villages have remained isolated from Nablus and from one another. A result of this physical isolation has been that their populations have spent considerable time trapped in states of limbo and uncertainty, and thus the conditions of life, as well as political and social developments within these individual communities, have been unique unto themselves.

Awarta is located southeast of Nablus city and has suffered a long history of isolation from other communities as well as aggression from the Israeli military and settlers. The Israeli settlement Itamar was established on the hilltops neighbouring the village and outposts of the settlement surround Awarta on three sides. The presence of Itamar has caused the village many difficulties, including limitations on the use of the village's wells and water resources as well as restrictions on construction and the expansion of generators and electrical lines. In more recent years the village has experienced increasing levels of aggression and regular acts of violence from settlers. To the west of Awarta is the village of Huwwara, through which the Nablus-Ramallah road runs, connecting the villages in between; it is the heavily patrolled lifeline of all that enters Awarta. Za'tara junction checkpoint is to the south of Awarta on the Nablus-Ramallah road and Huwwara checkpoint and military base are to the north at the entrance of the city of Nablus. The Awarta and Beit Furik checkpoints are situated on the remaining side streets leading into the village and are opened and closed, systematically, restricting the movement of people and resources in and out of the village. In this way the village is like many other communities in the Nablus region and throughout the West Bank. Prior to and throughout the second intifada Awarta had a reputation as a stronghold of resistance, and the village functioned despite its isolated conditions with improvised social programmes facilitated by PFLP (Popular Front for the Liberation of Palestine) activists. Eventually following the second intifada, the physical isolation of the village and the everyday experience of violence drove many members of the population apart, and rivalries between families and *hamula* began to emerge. In the years following the second intifada, settlers from Itamar have burned hundreds of Awarta's olive trees and the cars of many residents.

Burin is located southwest of Nablus on the opposite side of Huwwara village from Awarta. While the village is quite close to Nablus, it was cut off completely throughout most of the second intifada and remains under nightly curfew. As one resident told me, 'at night the village belongs to the soldiers.' A settler-only bypass road cuts through what used to be olive groves and homes on the southern edge of the village and the Israeli settlements Yitzhar and Bracha surround the village on the hilltops. Settlers attack the village on an almost daily basis, and the slopes and hills around the village are blackened from where olive groves have been burned. Nearly all of the windows in the village are covered by boards as a result of regular attacks. The centre of the village consists of many Ottoman era homes, and the surrounding hills and farmland are scattered with ancient ruins and tombs.

Assira Ash-Shamaleyya is located on the northern mountain of Nablus. Unlike the villages to the south and east of Nablus, Assira did not face the same levels of extreme poverty in the years following the second intifada. This was due to the absence of settlements in the area, which allowed the farmers to a large degree to retain control over their land, and also to the town being home to many Fatah officials who were formerly in diaspora and who were allowed to return after the formation of the PA. The village faced many hardships during the intifada including prolonged curfew and the occupation of the village's secondary school as a military command centre. Assira, meaning firewood, borders a dense pine forest overlooking Nablus on top of Mt Ebal, which has been declared a closed military zone and confiscated by the Israeli military base that is partly built on Assira's land. In the summer of 2020, following promises from the Israeli government to annex Area C of the West Bank, a new bypass road has been built over the lands of Assira, connecting the settlements of Itamar in the south of Nablus to Elon Moreh and settlements in the north. An outpost has also been extended over part of Assira's land, distancing it from

Fragmentation and Isolation in Nablus

the road and marking the beginning of a new settlement. The bypass road and outpost not only distance the population of the village from their lands but effectively cut Nablus off from the north and east of the West Bank.

Beit Furik is northeast of Awarta on the southeast edge of Nablus near the sprawling Askar refugee camp. Though a few local businesses exist in the village, it is completely surrounded by deep trenches dug at the beginning of the second intifada. There is no taxi service or paved road to Khirbet Tana, a former Bedouin village to the east of Beit Furik that extends into the desert of the Jordan Valley. An agricultural village consisting of a few scattered tents, the only permanent structure, is an ancient stone structure now used as a mosque. The village was destroyed six times between 2009 and 2011. Most of the Bedouin women and children live in temporary accommodations in Beit Furik, while a few men remain living in the one-room mosque and caves to look after livestock.

Sebastia in the north of Nablus is well known as a heritage site for its ancient ruins and the tomb of John the Baptist. The village built around a hilltop in the northern West Bank has thousands of years of history having been a political capital for the Roman Empire in the region and hosts the remains of a Roman amphitheatre as well as the well-persevered columns of ancient buildings. Over the years several development projects have focused on the restoration of historical sites as well as the conversion of some of the ancient homes into a hostel for travellers. Development projects which have been funded by the European Union and other governments have concentrated on the physical restoration of heritage sites while occasional tourists have contributed modest revenue to the town.

The decision to include Sebastia as part of this body of research came quite late in the process of editing and updating. I had spent quite a bit of time in the village in 2010 and 2011 due to some community projects that my friend was initiating, and at the time considered my stays there as a side project, despite spending many long nights sipping coffee and conversing with the people of the village. It was several years later when I would visit the village again to find considerable changes in the restoration of ancient structures and improved infrastructure to accommodate tourism, as well as a profound distance that had grown between the community and the heritage sites that their town was built on. In addition to the distance of the people living in the community an increased sense of poverty and desperation was visible in stark contrast with the physical features that had been the subject of investment. It was these changes and a concern for the well-being of the people that prompted my interests in the processes that had occurred there.

These satellite villages of Nablus are only a few of the different worlds existing in this region. Each area, neighbourhood and refugee camp have had its own unique experience and each have developed their own cultures through years of what I call fragmentation. This book is intended to illustrate the processes that have created fragmentation and to understand the meaning for the people living there by focusing on local examples. The pages that follow will detail a variety of ways that fragmentation has manifested over the late twentieth and early twenty-first centuries and how this has effected the existential realities for the people living out their lives in these spaces.

Interpretations of fragmentation

In the following chapters I explore the formations of geographical, political and social fragmentation in these communities, relying on historical and theoretical literature as well as my own ethnographic accounts. Physical fragmentation in terms of dividing the land itself and isolating Palestinians into various cities, villages and refugee camps as well as different regions and States at different points in history has created disconnect between populations and differentiation between people. As Palestinians have tried to express a collective political identity, various attempts to fragment, delegitimize and divide the people have led to a variety of struggles whereby political movements have sought to represent the population, articulating their own versions of political identity. Class formations have developed at different points also creating both indeliberate and systematic divisions, in the years since the second intifada class divisions under the PA have exasperated political fragmentation. Social controls regulate, administer and eliminate Palestinian narratives and lives to varying degrees. As different areas have become isolated from one another and political representation and identity become more ambiguous, social organization has become increasingly dependent on a community formations and more uniquely local expressions of identity have emerged.

Moving further I examine the roles of international development and aid organizations that have since the 1990s and increasingly during the early 2000s had profound effects in Palestinian communities as well as reorganizing local social structures. In looking at specific examples of foodways and agricultural movements I show how different communities were able to overcome imposed isolation by working together in collective gardening initiatives, as well as more recent threats to indigenous foods and resources. Narrative and shared histories work to solidify cohesion across various segments of Palestinian society and in otherwise divided communities, by looking at local examples of how residents of communities use narrative express a collective identity I illustrate some of the ways that communities counter the forces of fragmentation. Space in Palestinian communities is fragmented not only through physical divisions but also through keeping the populations in a constant state of disorientation and uncertainty through policies, regulations and various interactions and overlapping of Palestinian and Israeli social spaces. In observing and analysing the challenges and uncertainties that Palestinians must navigate to get through everyday life, I examine how they create meaning in their social worlds and rearticulate collective identity in changing situations.

Figure 1 Nablus cityscape with Mt. Ebal in the background. Photo by author.

2

Geographical fragmentation

Nablus loomed large in the eyes of its inhabitants, implanting in them a strong sense of regional identification and perhaps an exaggerated pride in those social practices they believed unique to their city.[1]

Beshara Doumani

Historical context of the land

The life experiences of Palestinians living in rural villages and urban centres of the West Bank have differed historically, and both have changed as the society and landscape have undergone drastic transformations over the last century. Palestinian cities were much smaller in the Ottoman and mandate periods, during which a majority of the population existed as an agrarian peasant society in the rural areas, while elite landowners and entrepreneurs resided in the cities. As a framework for identity, class was traditionally viewed as subordinate to religion, tribal affiliation and regional origin.[2] The colonial projects, starting with the British and continuing through the Israeli occupation, have used modes of capitalism as a model for controlling the population. Under British colonial rule in Palestine, attempts to stabilize capitalist systems in the region resulted in an increasing debt among the peasant communities due to their reliance on borrowing from landlords, which the British depended on as a political base.[3] The attempt to create a capitalist state while using non-capitalist peasant modes of production contributed to Arab labour not being integrated into the growing Jewish economy in mandate Palestine.[4] A response to capitalist colonialism in the Arab world during the early twentieth century, and to later agrarian reform policies, was the popularization of Leninist interpretations of Arab society in nationalist discourse.[5] During the first wave of Zionist immigration to Palestine during the 1880s (the First Aliyah), Jewish settlers often employed the indigenous Arabs as labour and security. By the Second Aliyah (1904–14), Zionist settlers had implemented policies against any integration of the Arab communities under the banner of Hebrew labour. This was a policy that the new wave of European Jewish settlers used not only to exclude the Arab population from employment and participation in social life but also to make a distinction between themselves and diaspora Jews who had previously immigrated from other countries in the region.[6]

The land of Palestine and its connection to the Palestinian people have undergone many physical, demographic and symbolic changes throughout the last century. Divisions in the land and divisions in the people have coincided through diaspora, development, siege and incursion. Likewise, as the land has been fragmented, the people have been as well. Different communities throughout the Levant, and the area that became Palestine under the British mandate, had previously existed essentially independent of one another. As opposed to the existence of any nationalist consciousness, religion, tribal affiliations and local traditions largely formed the basis for collective identity in the region during the Ottoman period, and local modes of production produced a state of relative autonomy in most areas, making the concept of nationhood of little relevance to the average individual. Relying on Ottoman-era literature, Beshara Doumani has illustrated the unique social and power relations that existed in the Nablus region. The poetry of Shaykh Yusuf emphasizes the 'cohesiveness of the region's social formation and the shared sense of identity among its inhabitants versus that factionalism of multiple territorially based centres of power'.[7] This highlights the alternative framework to the political hegemony of the centralized Ottoman government through the local solidarity of rural clans and influential merchants that represented the autonomy of Nablus. Unlike other urban centres such as Jerusalem and Hebron, Nablus not only had a large manufacturing base and was a key point in the networks of regional trade, but the city also had a strong connection with its hinterland. The villages that surrounded the city contained some of the richest agricultural lands in Palestine and the notable families in many of the villages consisted of the most prominent figures in Nablus society.[8]

Much of the standardized social structure in Palestine, particularly of that in terms of interactions between communities, was lingering results of the Tanzimat, Ottoman reforms issued between 1839 and 1876 aimed at modernizing the empire and integrating different ethnic groups. Under the Tanzimat, the religious institution was marginalized and lost much of its centrality in government.[9] Under Ottoman rule a sharecropping system known as *musha'a* tenure, in which land is allotted to all members of the community according to their ability to cultivate, was implemented in every village. In order to ensure that one family grouping was not given a better-quality allotment than another, the *musha'a* system divided the land into various plots throughout the village so that each family would receive an equal variety of terrain to cultivate, so as not to give one family the advantage over another. This was implemented to avoid creating class differences in the community. Land was redistributed among families on a yearly basis, but the right of a family to cultivate a specific portion of the *musha'a* was handed down from father to son.[10] Aside from a percentage of capital or produce that would be paid as tax to the Ottomans, the crops would be distributed within the community or in some cases taken to markets in urban centres such as Nablus and Jerusalem.

Traditionally, the basic social unit within a Palestinian village was based on *hamula* (clan).[11] *Hamulas* are patrilineal descent groups related by the fifth degree from a common ancestor.[12] The purpose of a *hamula* was to serve as a wider support system for loosely related families, as well as to defend their members, negotiate settlements and avenge deaths. Despite being subject to wars, reforms and the rule of multiple governments, rural West Bank villages did not change dramatically in terms of social structure until the late 1980s, during the first intifada, when emphasis pertaining to collective identity shifted away from *hamula* towards political struggle.[13] In this respect, the intifada was responsible for solidifying social cohesion between communities and integrating many rural areas into the collective Palestinian nationalist consciousness.

During Ottoman rule over Palestine the extent of autonomy differed drastically from one region of Palestine to another, and as early as the seventeenth century Nablus developed a reputation for being the most difficult area to control.[14] From as early as the nineteenth century Nablus has been referred to as *Jabal al-Nar* (mountains of fire). The epithet apparently originated from the legend that Napoleon's army was defeated by the populace of Nablus when they apparently burned the invading French soldiers alive by setting the forests and olive groves surrounding the city ablaze.[15] Nablus also played a leading role in the 1834 revolt against the invading Egyptian forces, the 1936–9 rebellion against Zionist colonialism and British rule, as well as both the first intifada in 1987[16] and the second intifada from 2000 to 2005.

By the time that the West Bank was occupied by the Israeli military in 1967, the landscape had changed drastically. Modernized infrastructure had been built and expanded in urban areas during British and Jordanian rule, and new market systems were established for moving fruits and vegetables grown in villages to other communities more efficiently. During the 1970s, mass migration of the labour force from rural communities and refugee camps to Israel to work on construction sites left a void in the peasant base that made up most villages, profoundly altering the social structure.[17] One of the first examples of grassroots mobilization in the West Bank that took place during the 1970s was the formation of volunteer youth camps organized in universities by leftist political movements (mostly the Communist Party, but the PFLP was involved as well). The aim of these camps was to create a replacement workforce to help farmers in rural villages who had been left short-handed by the migration of labour to Israel.[18] By the mid-1980s there was a grassroots network of organizations that had a popular base and were able to provide the basic services lacking in the community.[19] Later during the first intifada political movements were able to mobilize entire communities and came to replace the traditional elite structures that existed in many villages. As Hilterman describes, 'popular movements developed committees to provide education and basic services to the population living under the relatively lawless and economically deprived conditions.'[20]

During the first intifada, in order to crush emerging popular organizations, Israeli intelligence would frequently give backing the more conservative elements in rural villages such as landlords and the heads of *hamulas*.[21] The most profound example of this was the Village Leagues, which were, as Tamari describes, 'Israel's native pillar', consisting of groups of peasants led by clan and village leaders who were employed by Israel to act against the urban nationalists and cause chaos in small communities in order to stifle popular movements and sustain the 'traditionalist' village social order.[22] At the time of writing, there continues to be widespread opposition to popular mobilization, particularly in rural villages and refugee camps, from both the Israeli military and the Palestinian Authority. Julie Peteet notes that the most devastating acts of violence generally take place in villages and camps, so the violence is therefore 'somewhat class bound'.[23]

The Oslo Accords and what became known as the Oslo period (1993–2000) had profound effects on Palestinian society. The establishment of the PA and the setting up of state-like institutions instilled the idea among the population that sovereign statehood was imminent. The Oslo Accords began with the signing of the Declaration of Principles, in which Yasir Arafat and Israeli Prime Minister Yitzak Rabin agreed on limited Palestinian self-government and partial Israeli territorial withdrawal from areas of the West Bank and Gaza. Concerning critically important issues such as borders, refugees and East Jerusalem, which Israel annexed in 1967, it was essentially 'agreed to agree later'.[24] This created limited Palestinian autonomy but also closed off the Israeli economy to Palestinian workers who had worked as unskilled labour in Israel, which had constituted only source of income for the majority of employed Palestinians over the previous two decades. Despite an influx of foreign aid to support the peace process, this led to a rapid increase in unemployment among much of the population. Oslo 2, which was signed in Cairo in 1994, actually laid out the foundations for creating the PA as a transitional government and allowed for the return of Arafat and exiled cadres to the West Bank and Gaza. Many symbols of sovereignty such as ministries with letterhead, police, security forces and travel documents for Palestinians were also developed; however, without recognition from Israel any true autonomy has been limited at best. The Oslo Accords also divided the West Bank into three distinct areas of autonomy. Palestinians were given security and administrative control over the Area A, which comprises the urban centres excluding East Jerusalem. In Area B, the PA was given control of administrative affairs while the Israeli military retained control over security in Area C. This has left approximately 83 per cent of the West Bank under Israeli military control; this area surrounds 227 scattered cantons that constitute Area A.[25]

After the first intifada and with the implementation of the Oslo peace process, West Bank cities under PA autonomy have grown dramatically. As a result of settlement expansion further marginalizing rural villages and PA development in cities, a steady migration of young Palestinians from rural to urban areas has been a growing trend, and has in many ways left villages depleted of their more skilled and able labour or of highly educated individuals who could otherwise aid in development.[26] Many factors in the post-Oslo period, including limitations on Palestinian labour in Israel, increased military restrictions on the movement of people in and out of rural communities due to expanded settlements and international aid concentrated in Area A, have contributed to the deterioration of and eventual disappearance of some rural villages. In terms of political mobilization and social solidarity, during the second intifada many of the grassroots organizations that operated inside of Nablus area villages in order to provide services have disappeared, and what remains is an increasingly conservative, impoverished and isolated community relying once again on the traditionalist social structures.

Nablus during the second intifada

The city of Nablus is situated in a valley between the slopes of Mt Ebal and Mt Jerzim, and is historically the commercial centre of Palestine. Nablus's Old City has been inhabited by a diverse population since the Roman period, and contains several ancient mosques, churches and a Samaritan synagogue. The city has also been historically famous for the production of olive oil soap and is home to several soap factories that continue to produce soap using the original methods. Since the establishment of Israel in 1948, three refugee camps have been established in Nablus, and mass migration from area villages throughout the 1970s and 1980s has resulted in the city expanding dramatically in both size and population. Throughout the second intifada, the entire Nablus municipality remained under complete siege and travel in and out of the city was severely restricted, to the extent that people residing in various neighbourhoods and villages were unable to leave their areas. According to the Palestinian Red Crescent, Nablus was placed under complete curfew, meaning that residents were unable to leave their homes for 20 per cent of the time over the three-year period between 2002 and 2005.[27] The result of the siege and isolation on the different communities existing in the city, and to a much larger degree in the refugee camps and villages that surround it, has been that individuals have been forced to create logistical networks within their communities to trade basic goods and services in order to cope with the conditions imposed upon them. As members of communities with pre-existing social networks based on family relations, as well as the networks formed through political organization and economic necessity, individuals share distinct features of memory and identity through their communities. The city is divided into several distinct areas, including the three refugee camps inside the city limits. All of these regions consist of many neighbourhoods, each having its own history, interrelations and identity.

The Old City, where most of my time inside the city boundaries of Nablus was concentrated, is the historical centre of Nablus. With streets and building foundations dating to pre-Roman era, the Old City is the most impoverished neighbourhood in Nablus and the most devastated by Israeli attacks during the second intifada. The Old City was perpetually placed under curfew during the intifada and both Roman era sewage tunnels and holes made through walls either by the Israeli army or the residents themselves were used to smuggle food and supplies from one home to another. Such smuggling tunnels were the lifelines of the Old City, sustaining entire neighbourhoods during this period. Night raids and military incursions into the Old City continued frequently until 2012. During the intifada tall apartment buildings on the outskirts of the Old City, which were built on the slopes of Mt Jerzim, were frequently occupied by the IDF and used as command posts for weeks at a time, during which all of the residents of the building would be forced to wait together in one room on the ground floor while the military used the apartments as bunks for soldiers and the windows as points for sharpshooters to take aim. These apartment buildings continued to be regular targets of temporary occupation by the IDF during night raids conducted years after the second intifada. The terrain of the city itself was redefined in the ways that the Israeli military operated during the invasion of Nablus. As Eyal Weizmann explains, soldiers avoided using streets and alleyways in order to cause confusion. Instead of entering homes by conventional means such as external doors, they would whenever possible enter by 'punching holes through partition walls, ceilings and floors, and moving across them through 100-metre-long pathways of domestic interior hollowed out of the dense and contiguous city fabric'.[28]

The city of Nablus also contains three refugee camps: Balata, Askar (divided into two camps, old Askar and new Askar) and `Ayn Bayt al-Ma'. The refugee camps have also been at the heart of conflict with the Israeli military and within Nablusi society as well. The refugee camps have always faced a certain extent of social stigma from the wider Nablus community and have largely developed internally, as residents would seldom leave the camp. As displaced communities consisting of a mix of former cosmopolitan families from the coastal cities as well as former agricultural families from destroyed villages, the refugee communities were never able to fully integrate into Nablus. The generations born into a state of perpetual limbo inside the camps have created a unique collective identity for themselves through exclusion and neglect from many aspects of the wider Palestinian community. The refugee camps became important centres of resistance and symbols of the struggle of the Palestinian people during the first intifada. Even after the Oslo process and the creation of the PA, the camps remained marginalized, isolated and impoverished. During the second intifada the camps in Nablus were the staging ground for armed opposition to the Israeli forces and the majority of fighters who subsequently took control of the city during those years were residents of the camps. Following the outbreak of the second intifada until 2008, the PA security forces had little presence in Nablus nor did they have the ability to control the city. After the invasion and siege of the city, armed resistance groups, most notably al Aqsa Martyrs Brigades and to a lesser extent Hamas fighters, lost their ability to effectively attack the occupation forces. While the fighters to a large degree had lost the popular support of much of the Nablus population due to corruption and their gang-like behaviour, they continued to hold on to a degree of power, openly policing the city until 2008. The refugee camps remain isolated communities, cut off from other parts of the city and are still centres of conflict and regular night raids by the IDF.

Military bases with extensive surveillance equipment have been built by the Israeli authorities on both Mt Ebal and Mt Jerzim, which constantly look down on the city. Meanwhile drones fly over to take surveillance images and F16s break the sound barrier as a common form of harassment. This is a frequent occurrence but still causes the residents of Nablus to flinch with discomfort every time the thunderous sonic booms echo off of the mountains to either side of the city. A great deal of Mt Ebal is a closed military zone and older residents of Nablus will note that the top of the mountain was flattened and the terrain drastically shifted to make way for the large military base which is spread over half of the mountain top. It is widely rumoured in Nablusi gossip that part of the mountain has been hollowed out to make a storage centre for nuclear warheads. Surveillance is a fact of life in Nablus. During the second intifada assassinations of wanted fighters came in the form of entire city blocks being levelled by aerial bombardment. After Hamas took control of the Gaza Strip in June 2007, the PA, weakened from the second intifada, reshaped its political strategy in order to impose its authority in the West Bank. This had particular consequences for Nablus, as it was a Hamas stronghold in the West Bank. From 2009 the PA has made reforms for greater security collaboration with the Israeli military in the West Bank. The results of this experiment have been profound in Nablus. While the Israeli military has eased the siege on Nablus allowing limited goods in, many of the products entering the Palestinian market are of Israeli settlement origin, thus not sustainably stimulating the city's economy.

The two main checkpoints that restrict human movement in and out of Nablus are Huwwara to the southeast and Bayt Eba to the northwest, both of which exist more as permanent border crossings with small military bases attached and guard towers operated by snipers. Throughout the second intifada until June 2009 these were the only entry and exit points to Nablus and were closed to the majority of Palestinian traffic. Deep trenches and barricades had destroyed most other roads leading into the city. Smaller checkpoints exist at the entrances to the villages surrounding Nablus, largely sealing them off throughout the second intifada. Many of the villages that border Nablus to the south and southeast have remained sealed off beyond the intifada, causing high levels of unemployment and difficulties for youth seeking education.

Impact on rural areas

Rural communities, along with refugee camps, had been particularly marginalized and suffered greater levels of poverty than had urban areas prior to the signing of the Oslo Accords. Poverty in rural villages has increased dramatically since. After Oslo and the establishment of the PA in 1994, the West Bank was divided into different areas of autonomy. Cities that fell into Area A came under PA control while other areas remained under official military occupation. Because of this the experience of life in rural and urban communities became increasingly different. The daily experience of aggression perpetrated by Israeli forces also differed in various communities. This was particularly apparent during the second intifada, when villages were completely isolated from other communities and cities invaded and placed under long curfews. Hammami and Tamari have noted that during the second intifada the geography of physical fragmentation that was created by Oslo enabled Israeli forces to confine insurgency into Area A and control the Palestinian population.[29] The problems with physical isolation such as checkpoints and closure, as well as the dilemma of poverty in Area C villages, have made it difficult, if not impossible, for Palestinians living in villages to bring income into their communities. A 2010 report from the charity Save the Children UK found that the conditions of poverty in Area C[30] were significantly worse than those in the Gaza Strip.[31] There is a wide range of complicated factors that contribute to the situations of poverty and social deterioration in Area C, most obviously settlement construction and expansion and land confiscation. The refusal of the Israeli authorities to allow construction or the development of infrastructure is also a contributing factor to the deteriorating conditions in Area C.[32] Because the PA can only overtly operate in the urban centres, Area A, there are few employment opportunities in villages and they have been left largely neglected by the international aid which sustains and is distributed by the PA.

Getting by: Resilience in spite of isolation

The failures or resilience of specific individuals can impact on the collective narrative of a community. Trauma and suffering that are experienced on a personal level can also be recirculated and collectively experienced by a community. Life within the world of the isolated community can be shaped in ways that define that community by its residents, who, even under extreme circumstances, find ways to get on with their daily lives.

Checkpoints set up throughout the West Bank are a common feature of everyday life and perhaps one of the most well-known symbols of the occupation. Small checkpoints are strategically placed around every community in Nablus, restricting the movement of people and products, often inhibiting it completely. Larger checkpoints at the entrances of cities and along the separation wall cutting off Jerusalem and Israel proper from the West Bank resemble and operate more as international border crossings. Due to the placement of checkpoints and the specified routes that Palestinians must take, when travel is permitted, entire days are frequently spent attempting to move relatively short distances. Flying checkpoints, randomly set up along roads through the West Bank, which may appear one day and disappear the next, are also common. A study by the UN Office for the Coordination of Humanitarian Affairs (OCHA) counted a monthly average of 495 flying checkpoints throughout the West Bank between April 2009 and March 2010.[33] The result of closure throughout the second intifada has been that many Palestinians have not left their villages at all, even when siege was not implemented. Due to the difficulties associated with travel, between 2001 and 2004 85 per cent of Palestinians did not leave their villages due to the difficulty, contributing to the 70 per cent unemployment rate during that time.[34] In Nablus, the city as well as most small communities were under military siege throughout the second intifada and for most travel were not permitted at all. As a result those who did need to travel for work or education did so by taking dangerous routes through mountains.

Kennan had lived in Assira Ash-Shamaleyya all of his life, and enjoyed a comparatively well-paid job working in the PA bureaucracy, although over the years he had faced many challenges due to Israeli siege on the village throughout the second intifada. An avid cyclist, Kennan had multiple bicycles destroyed when stopped by IDF soldiers. He also had part of his home, which was positioned in Area B, demolished. When his wife became pregnant with their third child in 2006, Kennan knew that he would have to arrange some way to bring her to Nablus to give birth in the hospital. He had made arrangements for a Red Crescent ambulance to bring them from their home to Nablus via the Beit Iba checkpoint which, despite the fact that Assira directly borders the city of Nablus and has a road connecting the two, was the only way of entering the city from the north during the intifada. However, when the ambulance reached Beit Iba with Kennan and his wife who was in labour, they were turned away by the soldiers. After having the ambulance return them to their home, Kennan prepared his alternative ambulance, which was his donkey. Kennan took his wife and two smaller children by donkey through the pine forest on top of Mt Ebal, which was a closed military zone. By morning they were able to reach the hospital in Nablus in time for his wife to give birth.

Assira was under siege for five years throughout the second intifada, during which time education was severely compromised, as the Israeli army occupied the secondary school and turned it into a detention facility. As a result, all secondary school-aged students in the village had to take turns using the elementary school in the evenings after the smaller children had left. This caused many problems, as the facility was not physically made for larger students. The majority of the teachers in Assira were also from neighbouring villages and had to cross through the surrounding mountains in order to enter or leave the village, at risk of being detained, beaten or shot. Simple acts of resilience and just getting by under occupation have come to be a defining feature in the representation of the Palestinian people. While there are many impressive examples of communities maintaining social cohesion against all odds, there are as many in which community structure has fallen apart. Life in the isolated world of the Palestinian village can only be lived day-by-day; the uncertainty of life alone has contributed to the formation of a unique identity, particularly among Palestinians who grew up in isolation during the second intifada. The youth who have only experienced life within their community perceive their world through the lenses of that community; this has contributed to the development of social divisions between Palestinian communities, especially the rural and the urban.

Worlds of confinement

Through physically isolating individual communities from one another over long spans of time and effectively suffocating rural villages, the Israeli military has engaged in what has been a very successful programme of divide and conquer over the Palestinian population of the West Bank. Since the Oslo Accords divided the West Bank into different areas of autonomy, there has been a continuous attempt by the settlement movements to absorb as much land as possible while pushing Palestinian residents out. The geographic division of areas of the West Bank by the Israeli military and settlements has been referred to as a 'tiger skin' by the IDF, describing the random pattern of land classification that dictates which areas individuals are and are not allowed to move through. By allowing relative Palestinian autonomy to exist in a series of enclosed Bantustans, the Palestinian population inside of urban centres is allowed to enjoy some degree of normalcy within the confines of the city, while those living in villages are marginalized and for the most part lacking in employment, education and opportunities for growth. By the implementation of strict forms of isolation on cities and villages through checkpoints and military siege, as was the case in Nablus throughout the second intifada, Palestinian residents of isolated communities are not only inhibited from moving outside of their area but are alienated from their neighbours in other communities, causing social and political divisions over long periods of time. Israel's and the PA's drastically different treatment of different communities – cities, refugee camps and villages – has contributed greatly to the social fragmentation among Palestinians. The nationalist solidarity among the Palestinian people, which was emphasized by the first intifada, was a result of a highly diverse Arab population facing antagonism to a similar degree. Isolating different groups of people from each other and imposing a wide range of restrictions on various communities over the course of the second intifada have created a situation in which Palestinians living in different communities develop entirely different identities from one another and cannot relate to each other in a sufficient way to resist the occupation effectively.

3

Political fragmentation

Every aspect of life and culture among Palestinians has become uniquely politicized. Through shared histories, labels used by others and their respective situations of non-belongingness wherever they reside, their shared identity is a political one. Political movements have played important roles in social mobilization in Palestinian communities from the refugee camps to small villages, at times functioning as the only power structures that could provide for many communities. Political organizations have often, with or without legitimacy, laid claim to represent the Palestinian people and solidify Palestinian identity. During the first intifada, community solidarity was viewed as tied to the actions of political parties, though social cohesion rapidly deteriorated after and especially through the second intifada.

Historical background of the first intifada

The creation of a Palestinian collective identity to a large extent has been viewed as a response to colonial occupation and the expulsion of the Arab population from the land. The evictions that took place in 1948 displacing Palestinians from what became Israel did not differentiate between clan, class or religion, nor did the subsequent military ruling over the Palestinians who remained in what became Israel. The antagonism that is in one way or another shared by all Palestinians in occupied territories as well as those in diaspora developed into a nationalist consciousness through clearly defining them as a nation of people united by a common history.[1] During the first intifada, political movements based on liberation ideology and active resistance against the occupation represented Palestinian national identity. The first intifada was a result of grassroots mobilization that came to include every segment of Palestinian society. Individuals living in both urban and rural areas were incorporated into the uprising and women as well as men participated in the nationalist activities on a large scale. Different political parties operating within the various communities in Palestine formed committees and labour unions to provide support for the needs of the population. In the case of resistance activity, the different movements involved were formally organized under the Unified National Leadership of the Uprising (UNLU), which managed the mass mobilization of Palestinians to participate in civil disobedience and activism against the occupation. Shortly after the occupation of the West Bank and Gaza, Israel took some responsibility for maintaining certain civil institutions such as schools, although they were governed under military law. In the mid-1980s, during the time building up to the first intifada, schools and other institutions were systematically shut down and gatherings for educational purposes were declared illegal. One of the most significant tasks of popular committees on a local level during the first intifada was to provide education to youth in various communities, often incorporating the political ideology of the movement that the committee supported. Through the empowerment of union and labour movements, the communist parties organized much of the population against exploitive employers as well as the military occupation during the intifada.[2] The various committees that were developed through the intifada played a large role not only in uniting the population in resistance activities but also in providing services to communities, which was important in terms of development.[3] Tamari has linked the rural development that took place to the formation of grassroots agricultural development committees, as well as the role of women in rural societies to the actions of women's committees and trade union movements.[4]

Nationalist political movements in Palestine became representative of the Palestinian image and collective Palestinian identity. During the first intifada every aspect of everyday life for every Palestinian living inside of the territories was altered to encompass a political nationalist element of resistance. This process of nationalizing the individual's daily exercises, through discourse with neighbours and family, and incorporating nationalism into pre-existing cultural identities is what Jean-Klein labels 'self-nationalization'.[5] The mobilization that took place as a result of resistance to the occupation in many ways modernized and developed rural areas and united different Palestinian communities in nationalist activities. Slyomovics explains how the committees formed by the popular mobilization changed Palestinian society:

> Old forms of social organization dependent upon traditional hierarchies such as clan and family, the pre-eminence of notables, and the absence of women, have been supplanted by proliferating popular committees that organize and direct a spontaneous political upheaval of men and women, young and old.[6]

Pre-existing forms of social organization and the new social networks that developed through nationalist activities and mass organization have influenced one another in many ways. The political movements that created the social organization needed for resistance and provided support and development within communities fed off of the traditional social networks already existing within the communities where they operated. In many communities political movements have become linked to *hamula* and family connections, while in others political divisions became points of contention within the community. Political movements also formed new social networks through establishing committees, unions and resistance activity inside of communities, as well as establishing networks between communities with other party members and organizations.

Relations of political movements in communities

During the first intifada different communities experienced various levels of aggression and struggled in different ways, but political movements working within the communities struggled together towards a common Palestinian goal, though with different ideas of what the end result for a nation would look like. While Palestinians frequently reminisce about the first intifada as a time when the entirety of the people were collectively united, in fact there existed many different aims and goals that were imagined by various actors to be under the same flag.[7] Various Palestinian communities with different situations and needs or affiliated with different political movements take the common experience of antagonism to work towards the same goal of liberation but also work against each other in imagining different goals for what the end product of their struggle will be. After the establishment of the PA and the increase in isolation experienced by villages that fell under Area C, the types of aggression experienced by different communities became increasingly different and political movements competed with one another for power.

Political parties became fully involved in the communities in which they were based during the first intifada, acting as a replacement for government and becoming involved in every aspect of the lives of the public. Bashar, a former Fatah operative and now ranking PA official from the village Beit Furik, described how Fatah integrated itself into the social structure of his village and how, through proving itself able to manage the village, Fatah was able to gain legitimacy in the eyes of the population, progressing beyond the previous power relations that had existed in the village.

> In the beginning, the party was functioning as the shadow government of the Palestinian people through managing their daily affairs, their struggle and social life, but discreetly and away from the spotlight since national Palestinian action was prohibited. So when the party had to intervene, a well-known party member would make the approach as a personal one, but everyone would know that he is in fact speaking in the name of the party. The clan and tribe as source of power were stamped out.

As a political institution, taking power from the traditional structures in the village led to a period of modernization not only in terms of organization but also in the ways that people thought about infrastructure. Political parties did not only provide a legitimate platform for facilitating services, they also involved themselves in personal aspects that had previously fallen on the family and clan, such as feuds and divorce.

> The party would intervene in almost all cases basically to lift an in-justice. The party served as a valid replacement for the courts of law. In most cases people would go to the party when a problem happens, but the party could actually enforce itself in the problem was critical and could have some serious ramifications [...] By the end of the intifada the role of the party began to diminish, as party members began to abuse their status, and the parties drifted away from what they used to be, and the resurfacing of the clans by the second half of the intifada. All this led to the weakness of the role of political parties. Another observation was that clan and party disputes did in many occasions result in a split in one another.[8]

Marxist political parties such as the Palestinian Communist Party (PCP), founded in 1982 and renamed the Palestinian People's Party (PPP) in 1991, the Popular Front for the Liberation of Palestine (PFLP) and the Democratic Front for the Liberation of Palestine (DFLP) all combine an agenda for social transformation with the struggle against the occupation.[9] These political parties have a minority of support in Palestine compared to Fatah, but they still hold membership in the PLO and have members as leaders throughout the various structures of the Palestinian Authority. During the intifada in 1987 the PCP and other Marxist parties were, along with Fatah, part of the Unified National Leadership of the Uprising, which managed the mass mobilization of Palestinians to participate in civil disobedience and activism against the occupation. Through the empowerment of unions and labour movements, the communist parties organized much of the population against exploitive employers as well as the military occupation during the intifada.[10]

In order to illustrate the significance of political relations within communities in producing social cohesion, the socio-political context and history of the village Awarta are relevant. Awarta is unique in that it has a history of having been a stronghold of the Marxist political faction, the Popular Front for the Liberation of Palestine, and throughout the 1980s and 1990s the village had a reputation in the area, as well as with the Israeli military, of being a site of strong resistance. The presence of the PFLP as a political entity in the village, particularly during the first intifada, impacted heavily on the collective identity of individuals living in the community as well as on their ability to function as a community in spite of the complete disruption of everyday life caused by military siege. As in other communities, health clinics as well as agricultural committees, woman's working committees and trade unions were set up in order to compensate for the lack of civil institutions and infrastructure left in the wake of the Israeli response to the intifada. This type of grassroots mobilization not only allowed communities to function but also helped modernize Palestinian communities by involving the entire community in political and logistical organization. The committees and the collective organization of the public that developed during the intifada incorporated specific political principals, as well as the nationalist ones that were widespread at the time, into the public perception of community. In the case of Awarta, these committees were mediated by the PFLP, and the political movement's specific brand of Marxism-Leninism was worked into the everyday activities as well as their stories and artistic expressions. Throughout the first intifada and until recently, study groups were organized between village youth and political mentors in the community, who would ensure that the young generation knew the literature of the party.

In the case of Awarta, what made the village unique was that it had been united as a community in resistance and social construction through ideology. During the first intifada and the first years of PA rule this was not inhibited by the outside influence of military occupation or Fatah's monopoly on the political process inside of the West Bank. The PFLP lost a portion of its financial and political backing after the fall of the Soviet Union, and since the creation of the PA the PFLP and other leftist movements have been financially dependent on the Palestinian National Fund, which is controlled and distributed by Fatah.[11] After the establishment of the PA, social services that the PFLP had provided to some communities in the absence of institutions during the 1980s were supposed to be facilitated through non-governmental organizations (NGOs) and the PA. As in many other villages, the PA is not organized or effective in providing any basic services and those that are provided are done so largely through internationally funded NGOs. On a larger scale throughout Palestine, there is growing concern in the leadership of many local movements that, while the international NGOs that have replaced many local grassroots movements provide limited services, they do not mobilize the public.

> [During the first intifada] The clan and tribe were [marginalised] and no one could act based on his clan or tribe, it was the popular movement that is steered by the party [PFLP]. There was a very strong sense of unity in the village throughout the intifada, but near the end of it, the files opened on collaborators and traitors, and because there was no clear and organised way to handle such a delicate matter, resentment grew and everyone suspected one another [...] The mature and intellectual leadership was imprisoned by the Israelis which made the second line [of leadership] fill in their place sooner than they should and before they matured as leaders of the popular struggle. This led the people to drift away from the political parties, and weakened their power and influence.

> The political party was the defender and umbrella of its members, but after they became weak, people began looking for an alternative. And this was

the new [re-emergence] of the clan as a power holder. But still it took the political trend, [for example] a certain family affiliated to a certain political party, and then some kind of disturbance with one of its members takes place, so as a result the entire family would leave that party and join the opposing party as retaliation and to protect its interests [...] Early in the intifada, and up until it was almost over; people were so close to one another and the sense of cooperation was very obvious on all levels. But towards the end of it and due to all the previously mentioned slopes, people began to drift apart from one another.[12]

The Palestinian national consciousness that unified and became representative of the people was rooted in political liberation movements. In individual communities, particularly during the first intifada, the political movements were often recognized as the most legitimate power structure and became as much a part of the daily lives of the public as family and religion. Just as political movements came to embody and represent the Palestinian people as one, they also divided the people and communities. Abu Ahmad lives in Aqraba on the edge of the Jordan valley. He discussed the dynamics of family–party relations in his village in the context of isolation. Aqraba was also cut off from Nablus and the surrounding communities by the expansion of and regular attacks from Itamar settlement and the destruction of the main road connecting Aqraba to Awarta and Beit Furik in June 2006.

> During the first intifada the political parties were the ones in control, and in my town it was two political parties that dominated; Fatah and Hamas. So in the case of any dispute or so, it was the parties which would intervene and people would go to. The effect and leverage of the clan or tribe was diminished to the point you could say it didn't exist.

> Things got to the point that a certain problem that relates to the political parties could lead to a split in a family. Many families were split due to the fact that some of its members were affiliated to a party and the others to another one.

> In my town, the heads of Hamas and Fatah were actually two brothers. The parties were involved in every aspect of life, for example opening new water canals that the people wanted but parties had some issues with the matter relating to the source of the water or so which stopped the effort. And that also applied to the delay in the arrival of electricity to the village.

The parties would have a role in every problem or dispute, up to problems between married couples and marriage and divorce. Ethical problems and rogue citizens were all handled by the parties [...] The political parties would impose themselves but people got used to it and it became the norm.

During the second intifada the political parties lost the support of the community not only by competing with each other for power but also, as leaders were assassinated and arrested, the members who filled the power vacuum would often shift their agendas from resistance and community sustainability to their own ulterior motives. In this way the fighters affiliated with the political movements simply became armed gangs.

During the first intifada [there was] a sense of cooperation between the public, personal freedom was a non-existing concept and all was [focused on] the common good of the people. The say of the political parties word was taken strongly and rarely disputed.

In the beginning the political parties were honest and idealistically functioning, but as time went on and the parties began to compete in domination and number of members the cases of injustice and hypocrisy began to surface in a rapid speed. There were no standards to join the parties. And people began to join the parties for personal reasons of protection by the party since the clan protection is no more valid and enough. People who never had weight on the social scale and weren't respected became men of power due to their party positions. Corruption began to increase and peoples' trust in the parties began to diminish by the end of the first intifada.

Splits inside the party became a common thing as the clan and tribe began gaining back influence. Party leadership and fighting on it became a source of inner disturbances in the parties and the quest for party leadership to obtain their personal agendas through the party. All [of] this, drove the people to completely lose faith in the parties.

In the second intifada the 'relative' power came back to the tribe and clan, as the political parties began to take in consideration the will and impact of the clan. And through this phase the role of the party began to diminish. The domination of power during the second intifada was to the armed militias 'mostly thugs' and especially those of them who belonged to well-known and strong families. Commonly those groups would announce their affiliation to a political party or an armed brigade that is associated with a particular party.[13]

Surveillance under the PA

Shortly after Oslo, the PA established a security force of 30,000 police, filling in different positions of the various security institutions that were formed. Graham Usher argues that this size of force was not needed to facilitate the economic and social development of the 2.2 million Palestinians who fell under the PA's autonomy but to 'keep a lid on a people in the absence of such development'.[14] Agents of the security forces, as well as Fatah activists acting as de facto police, have been noted intervening in many situations to fight crime and solve family or clan disputes, as well as carrying out punishment for 'moral offences'.[15] Similarly, after the second intifada fighters belonging to the Al-Aqsa Martyrs' Brigades were absorbed into the PA security forces as they were reassembled. The Al-Aqsa Brigades were formed as a result of competition between various Fatah leaders and concern that Hamas was gaining political popularity among the more marginalized sectors of the population. Their militia-like behaviour became a principal element in the social breakdown and fragmentation that characterized the uprising.[16]

The Islamist movements, Hamas and Islamic Jihad, had only menial support during the 1990s and, along with some secular movements such as the PFLP, strongly opposed the Oslo accords.[17] Arafat's sidelining of the PLO in 1996 order to invest fully in the development of the PA towards an imagined statehood led to the disempowerment of the PLO and a perceived abandonment of refugees in diaspora.[18] Frustrations grew particularly after the start of the second intifada with Fatah and the PA's emphasis on institution building and negotiations with Israel which seemed to constantly backtrack on agreements. These developments in turn contributed to the growing support for Hamas, especially in less affluent communities, as well as resentment towards the PA and an increased political polarization in general.[19]

Throughout, and to a lesser degree following, the second intifada, armed groups representing different political movements would act as vigilantes loyal to leaders within their locale in enforcing rule of law, regulating against what they deemed to be inappropriate behaviour among individuals and taking what they wanted from local shopkeepers in the name of the resistance. This was the case in Nablus with the Al-Aqsa Martyrs' Brigades which commanded particular power in the refugee camps and less affluent neighbourhoods of the city. In 2000, after the outbreak of the intifada and siege was imposed on Nablus, it was the Al-Aqsa Brigades that burned out shops in the city that sold alcohol. Alcohol remained forbidden in the city, although there is no specific legal regulation against it. Similarly, as the intifada wore on and Hamas's popularity grew exponentially, businesses that were owned by Hamas supporters or were rumoured to support the organization were also targeted by the brigades. After winning parliamentary elections in 2006 and, with popular support, ousting the PA government in the Gaza Strip in 2007, Hamas supporters gained more local prestige in Nablus as well as positions in the municipality. This resulted in regular clashes between Al-Aqsa Brigades and Hamas fighters in the city, and eventual widespread political arrests of Hamas operatives and supporters by the PA security forces.

The village Assira Ash-Shamaleyya sits on the northern mountain of Nablus and is separated from the city by pine trees and an Israeli military base. Assira is one of the more affluent villages in the Nablus area. Several of Arafat's close cadres, who had previously been in exile, were resettled there in the 1990s after the formation of the PA. Issues of internal politics in the village are tense and complex, as they are in every community in Palestine. Since the 1980s the village has been politically divided primarily between PFLP and Fatah factions. During the local elections for power of the village council in 2006 there were violent clashes between the two factions, and the powerful families in the village were divided to the extent that politically active women were threatened with divorce if they would not withdraw support for certain parties. At the time of writing, the village council is controlled by Fatah. Abu Basel, a highly active PFLP member in Assira Ash-Shamaleyya, explained to me his views of the shifts in power relations in his village during the second intifada.

> [During the first intifada] The final say was for the political parties, and in that period and phase all clans dissolved in the bigger pot of the political movement. In Assira, and during the first intifada the three dominant political parties were 'Fatah, PFLP and the DFLP'.

Political Fragmentation 41

There was a committee to coordinate between all factions and through this committee the strength and impact of the parties got more established. If there was a problem it would be raised to the party and the party would raise it to the parties' coordination committee, depending on how big the problem is.

The parties were the governing power and did actually function as a government and would take role in everything including marriage.

People would resort to the parties because they have imposed themselves 'the party is the law' […] The parties had established committees of well-known people who [were] respected and loved [by the community] to intervene whenever needed. The party members were all model citizens and looked up to [by] the population. And through that they have forced their respect and authority onto people. As a direct result of the state of understanding and the popular direction towards the struggle for liberation, [there was] a unified spirit in the society.

As the intifada rolled on, the role of the parties began to shrink down and *hamula* and tribe began to climb up back again. This [was a result of] the decisions the parties took at the time, which led the people to react negatively and [lose trust in] the parties […] This wave of people [losing trust] in the parties started from within the parties themselves, as the leadership of the parties outside of Palestine no longer supported the party inside with the same momentum […] And as a result [of] this crack within the party itself, people and the party members themselves began to lose trust in the parties and began to [become] driven away from them and [express] visible appearance of the opposition to the PLO even from within […] There was [sense of surprise expressed by] the PLO members inside [of Palestine, about] the decisions taken by the PLO in the outside [of Palestine] which led to a [dispute] in the popular movement […] The parties became different than they used to be, [they] began looking for quantity instead of quality. Recruitment methodology became different and the quality of the members became [worse].

During the height of the second intifada the PA was practically paralysed but still its security bodies were still functioning but on a very limited basis. Armed groups [emerged] that used the names of the parties and the struggle against occupation [for their] own interest by [engaging in act of extortion and intimidation in the village], which lead to a major state of lacking a reference to count on in that phase […] The phenomenon of families breaking up [for] political reasons was very obvious in our town as the biggest clan got split in half over this. 'PFLP/Fatah'

In Assira, as in other communities, the roles of political movements, which during the first intifada had been the driving forces of cohesion and solidarity within the community, had diminished and the community looked to more traditional and seemingly stable structures available to them. As people lost trust in the political parties and armed gangs grew in power, divisions grew, even within families and clans.

The social organization which developed through nationalism and provided support and basic needs in isolated communities in lieu of a properly functioning infrastructure has deteriorated and given way to traditional structures that had previously existed in the community. Hammami and Tamari note that the 'establishment of the PA and their substantial armed security apparatus have greatly weakened the social networks' that were formed by the popular struggle in Palestinian society.[20] The situation in the West Bank under the control of the Palestinian Authority and the fragmentation of the social networks that once created the solidarity reflective of a collective nationalist identity are comparable to situations that have arisen in many post-colonial states undergoing transitional periods. In the Palestinian context, however, ongoing colonial occupation overlaps with a post-colonial government apparatus. This situation has resulted in widespread disillusionment within the PA, though as a result of intimidation and dependency the public that had previously been politically mobilized is now largely silent. As Frantz Fanon describes when discussing the national consciousness in post-colonial Algeria,

> Instead of being the all-embracing crystallization of the innermost hopes of the whole people, instead of being the immediate and most obvious result of the mobilization of the people, will be in any case only an empty shell, a crude and fragile travesty of what might have been […] the nation is passed over for race, and the tribe is preferred to the state. These cracks are the edifice which show the process of retrogression, that is so harmful and prejudicial to the national effort and national unity.[21]

Fanon illustrates the failures of the post-colonial state, emphasizing the decline of the solidarity that had brought the Algerian public together. While traditional forms of social organization have survived and coexisted with the 'revolutionary culture' that was forged through the experience of Israeli antagonism and symbolized through a nationalized Palestinian collective identity, the advent of the PA has divided the Palestinian people, causing a deterioration of the unity that created it. The political fragmentation and divisions that have grown in communities have created a dependency on traditional social structures that pre-existed the nationalist unity, as they are all that remain in small communities to provide logistical support. The manifestation of institutionalized Palestinian-on-Palestinian surveillance has impacted on individuals' willingness to be openly involved in political activity, according to Usher:

> The emergence of an increasingly authoritarian PA has contributed to a process of depoliticization of Palestinian society in which many of its most able members have 'collectively withdrawn', reverting to individualistic or clan-based (rather than political) solutions for their needs and aspirations. This is not only regressive in itself, but erosive of the essentially modernist political national Palestinian identity that the PLO – its political factions and for all its faults – had brought into being.[22]

Issues of internal Palestinian surveillance have greatly increased paranoia and distrust within communities and have contributed to the growing collapse of community solidarity, particularly in rural villages and in the larger Palestinian community as a whole. As Usher and Tamari both noted above, individuals relate to the traditional forms of social organization that are more available to them in the absence of strong political organization. The weakening of central institutions during the second intifada contributed to what Jamil Hilal has described as a reinvention of kinship and locality-based associations and an emergence of 'politics of the local' which has enabled patriarchal relations and devalued notions of citizenship and law.[23] Because of the physical isolation of rural areas and absence of services facilitated by the PA, clan-relations had taken hold in West Bank villages leading to more local notions of politics and social organization.[24]

Awarta became well known in the late 1980s during the first intifada. This was initially due to the village being cut off from its surroundings by Israeli forces, as it was both a hot spot for resistance and a supply line of militancy in Nablus. But what made Awarta different was that it became something of a fortified enclave that remained cut off from Nablus and the surrounding villages. Nevertheless, it still managed to maintain its structural integrity as a self-sufficient community until midway through the second intifada, through community solidarity and support for the PFLP, or at least those members who led the village during the 1980s and 1990s. After Oslo, conditions in the village remained static due to its location in Area C and the neighbouring settlement Itamar. Several attempts have been made to upgrade the village's electrical grid, which was built in the 1970s, although the Israeli military has never allowed this. Many residents of Awarta have also complained of neglect from the PA due to Awarta's leftist history. Early on in the second intifada the leadership in Awarta set up backyard gardening initiatives but these ceased in 2004 when much of the leadership was imprisoned and cohesion fell apart.

> [In Awarta] The PFLP had the greatest impact of all, and would have a hand and a say in everything up to a point, that it was the only one [voice] in all matters. Since the courts of law were [irrelevant], after the Israeli occupation, people wouldn't follow the usual steps if there was any dispute and would go to the party rather than go to the courts. This relates to everything, even to marital issues between couples if one of the family members saw that this could escalate and asked the party to intervene.

> The intifada started as a popular movement, and everyone cooperated together as in the first intifada. But the second intifada was militarised and this means that the key players were those who held arms, towards the end the fighters were not working for resistance but for themselves.

> During the second intifada also, the clan surfaced back again much stronger and with the existence of the PA, mostly the clan was made as a main factor during the PM elections, as people would vote according to the clan rather than the political affiliation. In addition, many of the party members and party figures joined into the PA which took them [out of] the political arena which the people [were] used to have them in. This contributed to the weakening the political parties and their role.[25]

The PFLP was strong symbolically in Awarta in that they were organized in transmitting their ideology to the public during the 1980s and early 1990s. Youth in the community were indoctrinated in the literature and ideals of the movement through regularly organized meetings with tutors, and they would be mobilized in grassroots activities ranging from community restoration projects, helping local farmers and resistance activities against the occupation. These activities were all facilitated through the PFLP and provided a clear social and political identity to those involved through community action. As one resident, Tariq, told me:

> We learned about George Habash before we learned about Islam [...] In every village at the time [1980s] different political parties managed various aspects of life in the community, what made Awarta different was that the community stood behind the party completely. If someone were to hand out the literature of another party in Awarta, they would be beaten up very quickly.

The social networks created by the PFLP and other political movements in different communities kept the population involved in politics in Palestine and grassroots activities in their communities, and were important in maintaining community cohesion through the difficulties of occupation. Awarta is unique in having this history with a specific political movement, which is still present, but in practice their actions in the community no longer involve mobilizing the population and are largely symbolic. Until just after the second intifada, Marxist study groups had been taking place in the village but other activities that promote mass mobilization and community development are no longer organized.

Prior to and throughout the first intifada, Israel implemented harsh policies of censorship on theatre and published material coming from the Occupied Territories, as part of a larger programme aimed at restricting the circulation of information and cultural identity.[26] Censorship was also applied to political graffiti, which was strictly forbidden and during the first intifada it was often painted over by Israeli soldiers soon after its application.[27] Graffiti was used as a means to contest and defy Israeli surveillance, in addition to sending messages to the community such as news and political commentary.[28] Political graffiti from throughout the first and second intifadas remains faded on the walls in nearly every Palestinian village, and serves as a reminder of the current struggles against the occupation and between political factions. Since the end of the second intifada and Hamas establishing political autonomy over Gaza in 2007, the PA security forces have dramatically expanded operations throughout urban areas of the West Bank. Since 2009, in Palestinian cities such as Nablus, PA security forces paint over graffiti left by Hamas supporters or anything that is critical of Fatah in a similar way to the way the Israeli military had done during the 1980s and first intifada. This type of Palestinian-on-Palestinian censorship and surveillance has been in place since the creation of the PA in 1994 but has increased considerably in the years that followed the second intifada. Since its implementation as a quasi-state apparatus, the PA has been allowed to exist through maintaining security cooperation with the Israeli military, and its role has been overwhelmingly focused on security and intelligence gathering. While the PA has been successful in terms of creating jobs in urban areas, this has come at a cost to rural villages in Area C, which have been left physically isolated because of the occupation and are suffering from the mass emigration of young and skilled residents to urban centres. As of two decades after the signing of Oslo, nearly all employment in the West Bank is facilitated through the PA, either directly or through one of its umbrella organizations.

Fragmented political identity

Political fragmentation in the Palestinian context is characterized not only by the split in political movements, most notably the division between the PA in the West Bank and Hamas in the Gaza Strip, but by a disillusionment with any political leadership which has grown since the second intifada. Isolation and divisions between various communities resulted in modes of social organization to be thrown back onto local structures in the absence of trust in the PA or strong political movements.[29]

Hamas had gained wide support in the occupied territories in large due to frustration and disillusionment with the PA and the failing Oslo process. Hamas had rejected the Oslo process from the beginning as well as the formation of the PA, insisting that resistance to occupation should not be replaced by State-building. The movement gained increasing legitimacy amid constant Israeli backtracking in agreements with Fatah and the PA. Following the death of Arafat in 2004 and the election of Mahmud Abbas in 2005, Hamas ran, and won, in the 2006 elections of the Palestinian Legislative

Council.[30] Having won the majority of seats in the PLC, Hamas would have had the right to form a new PA government, an outcome that Israel and the United States found unacceptable.[31] Perceived US military support for Fatah after the 2006 elections significantly contributed to support for the armed clashes that ousted Fatah from Gaza and more widespread distrust of the PA.[32]

Palestinian culture since 1948 has come to be represented by nationalist aspirations and resistance through the shared history of the people. Regarding the socially conservative nature of Palestinian political culture, Lisa Taraki has observed that

> despite the spontaneous and organized rebellion and the hegemony of discourses of liberation and resistance [...] Ideologically, conservatism has found expression in a nationalist discourse which has as its referent an idealized stable rural society unsullied by the violence and dislocation brought upon it by colonial rule.[33]

Through the mobilization leading to the first intifada, Palestinians defined their common identity as a nation through their socially constructed sense of belonging to a common community. With the creation of the PA in the 1990s, the population acquired a pseudo-state capable of monopolizing violence as a form of control and distributing some services but with limited political power and without representation of the people as a nation.[34] The popularity of conservative movements in Nablus during the years since the Oslo process has been a contributing factor in the splintering of political identity within the city and surrounding villages, which has in turn resulted in deterioration of solidarity between communities and a reliance on local forms of social organization. This shift has subsequently been accompanied by the marginalization of nationalist consciousness in the absence of the PA or official institutions providing popular or meaningful representation.

Tamari has noted the failures of the left to act in response to the rise of conservative movements[35] and argued at the end of the first intifada that 'the left should have struggled to redefine the cultural domain in public life, particularly by supporting educational reform, press freedom, and creative forums of popular culture'.[36] The type of grassroots mobilization required to bring communities together and motivate the public to develop and maintain small villages, such as was the case during the first intifada, has been largely absent since the Oslo period. The increase in international NGOs providing services to communities that were once provided by mobilized members of the community is also a contributing factor to the growing crisis of apathy. A majority of existing development projects have since been facilitated through NGOs often consisting of outsiders and internationals. Naseef Muallem argues that the left has lost its base among the youth by refraining from electing new blood, and that the leadership of leftist parties has never adjusted to the political circumstances of an authoritarian PA, which requires a new young leadership that is capable of carrying out above-ground political work.[37] The inaction of the PFLP in the case of Awarta and of other movements in other communities to facilitate community programmes aimed at basic assistance and development in small communities prevents them from instilling the nationalist political identity that had existed in the past, and has led to a diminishing of solidarity within communities.

Redefining class formation

Historically, the communities residing in the mountains of the West Bank have been agrarian peasant societies with community relations largely based on kinship and local clan relations. In contrast, the port cities of the coast had a long cosmopolitan history of mixing of cultures and interaction between artisans and merchants.[38] During the late Ottoman and Mandate periods developments in new class formations had already started to change local social structures in Palestinian communities. Lisa Taraki has examined middle-class formations that developed in Ramallah and al-Bireh during the turn of the twentieth century due largely to residents emigrating to the United States and then returning. Patterns of emigration and connections through Quaker networks and Protestant universities enabled former peasant families to buy land and establish leadership roles in the community, integrating Ramallah in both regional and international influence. New class formations not only changed the economic and political positions of some communities, but also drew distinctions and in some cases created unintentional divisions and animosity.[39] While social changes and class formations during early twentieth century have had lasting effects on community structure, the interruption of the Nakba overshadows many of the prior developments in Palestinian urbanization.

Just as the development of a formerly peasant middle class and urbanization changed the dynamics of Palestinian communities, the return of formerly exiled Palestinians after Oslo contributed to divisions in communities and constituted the creation of yet a new middle class. The 'returnees' who were generally well connected in Fatah and the PLO predominantly made up important positions in the newly established PA, while locals who had often been long-serving activists in communities frequently formed the bases of NGOs.[40] Elite Palestinians returning from exile to take up positions in the PA administration were also often viewed as out of touch with local issues and criticized for decadent behaviour. Perceived class differentiation between 'returnee' and 'local' residents has at times been a source of tension as well as a distinction in local identity in some communities.

Since the development of Ramallah as a de facto capital of the PA, the town has become synonymous with an upper-middle class that has grown through the institutions funded by donor aid and isolated from much of the rest of Palestinian society. The development of a technocratic urban middle class under the PA is a feature common in post-colonial client states. During the 1980s, when the nationalist mobilization that eventually resulted in the first intifada was emerging, new social formations that led to the establishment of popular committees brought about social changes in terms of class interactions in addition to political mobilization. Urban professionals with ties to the various political factions established agricultural relief and heath relief committees that focused on establishing clinics and self-sustainable farming in the rural villages, as well as health education and backyard farming projects in the cities and refugee camps.[41] This was vital to the transformation of the rural landscape in that many of the health committees involved female doctors who were tied to women empowerment projects. The organizational development also built connections between the urban professionals and the populations of rural villages and refugee camps, which the former urban elite had not previously done.[42] This marginalized the old elite, which was tied to the traditional social formations of leading notable families within specific regions.[43] However, the elements of the pre-existing elite have remained and rivalries between families and, particularly since the end of the first intifada, clan-relations have continued to fragment Palestinian society and undermine nationalist collective action.[44] Since the formation of the PA a greater separation has developed between the new middle class and more marginalized sectors of the Palestinian population. This is due largely to overdevelopment in Ramallah and to a lesser extent other urban centres, and an inability to promote development and provide for basic needs in the rural areas. The new urban middle class is largely isolated to Ramallah or the other cities, and views the occupation but does not experience it to the full degree of the rest of the population. A sense of alienation and increased social stigma has contributed to the growing disparity between the urban middle class under the PA and the larger population, particularly in rural villages and refugee camps, which face increasingly deteriorating conditions.

As in post-colonial client states, the main aspiration of an elite and administrative middle class is not the liberation of the society but the accumulation of power and capital. Frustrations among many in Nablus have suggested that in the case of an administrative middle class that has developed in the West Bank and prospered under the PA, recent social conditioning has occurred that separates them from the rest of the Palestinian community. The experiences of dispossession and occupation are felt differently across Palestinian community; the disparity which has grown between an administrative middle class and other segments of the society has increased the social distance they do not share in the same struggles or everyday life with the rest of the people. Elite and perceived Western comforts can be enjoyed within the confines of urban centres such as Ramallah, separating them further from the deteriorating conditions of the villages and refugee camps. Resentment and social stigma between groups of urban Palestinians and rural or refugee Palestinians had previously existed in the West Bank but have increased to the point that differences in social identity outweigh a cohesive nationalist identity. This new class difference constitutes a greater level of social fragmentation in Palestine, as the affluent few speak for the entire community but are not representative of them. Frantz Fanon has made note of the deteriorating nature of the post-colonial middle class:

> The traditional weakness which is almost congenital to the national consciousness of underdeveloped countries [...] is also the result of the

intellectual laziness of the middle class, of its spiritual penury, and of the profoundly cosmopolitan mould that its mind is set in.[45]

The presence of the PA as a bureaucratic instrument collecting international aid and distributing it throughout its institutions, all the while protected by its security forces, has developed this urban middle class by way of the creation of large-scale employment for a limited and privileged segment of the population, although the overwhelming majority of this segment is either unquestioningly supportive of PA policies or politically silent.

Colonial rule under the British Mandate saw the repression of the middle class and attempts to divide the population along local and religious lines, common in the creation of client states. Under Israeli rule, the Palestinian populations within Israel are maintained as an under-class marginalized on multiple levels as class stratification is mediated by institutionalized policies aimed at structuring inferior economic positions and dehumanizing indigenous people.[46] The class differentiation that has emerged in the occupied territories since Oslo in the 1990s shares similarities post-colonial client states, but situated within a settler-colonial structure, as Israel continues to expand settlements in the West Bank selectively extending sovereignty, and maintain control over resources, labour and space. Class divisions are used across spaces and narratives dividing Palestinians further into different categories in terms of economics as well as the right to exist in certain places.

Reimagining solidarity

Notions of Palestine as a collective consciousness and identity are frequently associated with imagery of occupation and a nation denied. Solidarity which was formed around the experience of dispossession, suffering and collective antagonism came to represent an expression of political identity through resistance. The shared memory of a history interrupted and stories of Ottoman and Mandate Palestine become symbols of a common imagination. Issam Nasser points out that the Nakba represents more of a rhetorical shift in the expression of a collective identity than a beginning or end to it. While the traditional local aspects of Palestinian population centres were lost, the refugee experience became a distinctive feature of Palestinian narrative and identity.[47] The collective identity centred around the refugee narrative dominated political discourse until the Oslo process in the 1990s. Because the Oslo Accords focused specifically on the populations of the West Bank and Gaza in developing a concept of Palestinian citizenship, Palestinians residing outside of these areas became excluded in subsequent discourse aimed at defining a Palestinian political collective.[48]

While every aspect of daily life in Palestine is distinctly politicized as a result of the experience of life under the occupation,[49] the layers of divisions which have grown through the institutionalization of Palestinian society have resulted in a growing rejection of previous political discourses. In the geographically fragmented Palestinian cantons of the West Bank, political movements took on the roles of representing communities and, to some degree, of attempting to provide civil institutions and basic infrastructure. In some cases political movements created solidarity within communities and held the population together through adverse periods. In other cases different groups competing for power and the actions of armed militias associated with the parties drove communities apart. As the PA was formed to normalize the political and social situations in the context of continued occupation, discontent with the status quo and worsening conditions has grown. The lack of an effective legal system or trusted representation has caused people, particularly in rural areas, to turn to personal relationships and less accountable alternative ways of creating social order.[50] As geographical fragmentation intensified following the second intifada and settlements continue to expand, rural communities have become neglected by the PA institutions and further marginalized. Political fragmentation has developed on several levels; competition between political actors, widespread dissatisfaction with the authoritarian rule of the PA and corruption within the political parties and their abuse of the public have all led to a general distrust in political leadership.

A generation of Palestinians who have come of age in the years since the second intifada disillusioned by corrupt and hopeless politics and divided under the pressures of fragmentation has given way to a new solidarity in popular rejection of the old political discourses and is pushing a new grassroots momentum independently of political parties. Displays of solidarity which were seen across the West Bank, Gaza and throughout Israeli cities since May 2021 constitute a major change in the political collective of Palestinians in terms of a coherent unity not displayed since the 1936 uprising[51] and a rejection of the political authorities is a historical turning point and necessitates a rearticulation of Palestinian identity. At the same time, intensely violent repression from both the Israeli and Palestinians authorities in response to demonstrations of solidarity illustrates not only the impressive acephalous nature of such movements but also a very real fear of the public uniting. A new collectivity and cohesion built across different groups of Palestinians divided by territory, politics and class have come together in an attempt to reinvent a cohesive voice as one people in redefining collective goals to end an unsustainable situation of division and fragmentation.

Figure 2 Al-Nasr mosque in the Old City of Nablus. Photo by author.

4

Social fragmentation

Seemingly irreversible forces of fragmentation – class and generational tensions, political disputes over the role of armed groups, power struggles between and within factions, turf battles between institutions, and deep estrangement between the nearby refugee camps and the city – have taken root in Nablus and threaten to cause an implosion at any moment. At the same time, Nablus is being quickly transformed demographically and physically as a result of three Israeli policies: land grabs for building the isolation wall and expanding the illegal Jewish settlements; the separation of the various Palestinian population areas through severe restrictions on movement between them; and, not least, the separate and unequal treatment of Palestinian cities with Nablus at one end of the spectrum and Ramallah on the other.[1]

Beshara Doumani

The social breakdown that has enveloped Palestinian society exists beyond the political context and can be understood through looking at shifts in popular perceptions and disjuncture of cohesion within communities. The villages in Area C south of Nablus have experienced increasingly difficult circumstances of isolation resulting from changing military orders and frequent attacks from nearby settlements. These communities and others inside of Nablus have also become isolated due to differing treatment from the larger Palestinian community itself. Various strategies such as long-term isolation through siege, strict controls on access to resources and instrumentally disrupting social relations on a community and family level have been imposed with the aim to stifle Palestinian civil society, but have also had deeper affects in impacting concepts of community and the individual sense of self. Through examining the recent history of systematic geographic, political and social fragmentation, shifts of consciousness impacting on the notion of collective identity can be traced and understood.

Palestinian society has been subjected to multiple levels of fragmentation, not only in terms of the physical division of the land imposed by the Israeli occupation and political divisions between rival factions, but also through varying processes of social fragmentation within and between communities. Settlement construction and military restrictions isolate communities from one another by limiting the movement of people, products and information. The development of the Palestinian Authority as an authoritarian state apparatus and its limited ability to provide services to the population have increased the division between political factions and caused a deterioration in social conditions in marginalized areas that remain isolated due to continued occupation.

Prior to fundamental changes in the social structures of communities resulting from the creation of Israel in 1948 and the occupation of the West Bank and Gaza in 1967, individuals, particularly those living in rural Palestinian communities, would have tended to identify more strongly with local structures based mainly on family and community relations within a certain area and regional affiliation rather than a national consciousness.[2] The grassroots mobilization that came to characterize the first Palestinian intifada incorporated all segments of the society, including women and youth from both rural and urban backgrounds, in nationalist activities such as civil disobedience and public demonstrations as well as restructuring and developing the modes of organization of the society itself. The mass mobilization and new social organization created a sense of solidarity among Palestinians suffering through common experience. The popular uprising was built on the development of committees within communities that coordinated resistance activities, as well as establishing medical clinics and providing education and development programmes in rural villages.[3] The new networks of social organization that developed through grassroots mobilization within communities transformed the society and heavily emphasized themes of resistance, community development and a nationalist pan-Palestinian identity. Increasingly, since the advent of the PA, and particularly since the second intifada, the political structures created by the Oslo process have symbolically abandoned the politically active base of the occupied population by not accepting a role in the uprising, and a crisis of social fragmentation has become increasingly prevalent. The result has been deteriorating social conditions in many communities, causing individuals to revert to traditional modes of social organization. Much of the political fragmentation and disillusionment with political solutions is due to the increasingly controlling nature of the PA and the absence of any strong political alternative. The lack of legitimacy of the PA and various local councils perceived by much of the population, and their relevance in the lives of ordinary Palestinians, forces people to focus on more organic structures within their communities. What remains in most cases is a reliance on kinship relations in facilitating everyday social needs and acting as structures for dealing with community problems.

Social structures and fragmented identities

Political movements had become prominent features in Palestinian society in the 1970s and 1980s, mobilizing communities and maintaining hegemony over every aspect of political and social life. In the 1990s the place of political movements in the social life of Palestinians weakened considerably as political emphasis shifted from mass mobilization to diplomacy, which allowed pre-existing social formations to reassert themselves as the main forces for maintaining cohesion.[4] The absence of an authentic indigenous state authority in the West Bank and Gaza since 1967 has, as Lisa Taraki notes, created a vacuum in which the relationships between kinship and politics developed differently than in other Arab societies.[5]

While the role of *hamula* has been largely symbolic in the later part of the twentieth century, in that elders were only convened on ceremonial occasions, Taraki notes a recent 'revival of the *hamula* structure in the areas of social support and political life.'[6] Kinship ties and links to *hamula* have been, in most Nablus-area communities, the mediators' choice for solving disputes and issues within the community. This is because of both the perceived ineffectiveness of the PA legal system and police force, which in Area C villages is unable to operate regardless, and the immediate access to kin structures that have long held a role in dictating matters at the local level. The main exceptions to this have been local mediation through political parties prior to the second intifada, and in many villages kinship links were integrated to a degree into political movements. Kin relations in terms of extended family and *hamula* constitute an important part of rural Palestinian culture. Most villages are made up of between two and five *hamula*. As Heiberg and Ovensen note, family relations in Palestinian society intersect all levels of stratification and create 'a complex pattern of socioeconomic interdependence'.[7] Through marriage within a *hamula*, families form alliances with one another and villages are able to continue traditions, local identity and land ownership. The structure found in kinship and clan relations also compensate for the absence of security or a state authority.

While conversing over coffee in Awarta, Tariq spoke critically of the disengagement of local youth from community work and their shifting interest in accessing new outside worlds, something which I found understandable considering they had grown up isolated under siege. Though for the most part the youth or indeed any average person in such villages could not afford to visit places such as Ramallah which was considered both remote and luxurious.

> It is a joke to say that the siege is lifted. Look at Huwarra, Beit Iba (the major checkpoints cutting off Nablus), you can drive through them today after years of being closed in, but there are still armed [Israeli] soldiers standing guard and military bases right there to jail and interrogate us! It is like a faucet, the checkpoint is open today, but people forget, it can close any moment they want. And if they want you they will take you away!

As we talked we were joined by a group of young men, mostly in their late teens, who seemed primary concern over availability of prospective marriage partners, as well as expressing a curiosity about the world beyond the realms of their village and the West Bank. I was interested in learning more about their preferences and anticipation so I tried to stimulate conversation in jest by asking them what their criteria for marriage were. They argued and joked amongst themselves as to if it would be possible to find a partner within the confines of the village where most families knew one another, often too close for comfort. All of the group had grown up in Awarta and only rarely had the opportunity to venture outside of the village during their lifetimes, although a few of them did speak of aspirations of travel. While they imagined travelling to historical Palestinian and Israeli cities as well as to the outside world, they also expressed an affinity for their village and a desire to return and maintain their family structure. As the fantasized some insisted on marrying within the village while others suggested that it would be acceptable, or even preferable, to find a partner from elsewhere in Palestine or even outside, so long as they returned to the village. When I enquired as to why they looked at one another puzzled, and then concluded that otherwise their families would end.

The attitude of the young men expresses a sense of safety found within the confines of one's own community as opposed to an outside world of uncertainty. It also has implications that are tied to kinship. Penny Johnson has explored the links between kinship-based marriage arrangements in Palestinian communities as they are pursued for practical purposes.[8] According to Johnson, marriage arrangements between first cousins, which are particularly popular in rural villages, reinforce kinship solidarity and provide protection for individual, family and community survival. Fragmentation and the isolation of communities have reinforced the importance of kinship for family and individual survival and welfare while weakening other spheres of public action such as political mobilization.[9] Despite the recent re-emergence of the role of kinship structures replacing political movements as structures for mediating hegemony, Johnson argues that kinship mediates rather than conflicts with national identities. Solidarities and identities that exist and are expressed through kinship constitute an important part of Palestinian national identity.[10] Symbolic economies are the product of capital created through kinship relations in Palestinian communities, which can in turn respond to the systems of domination to which they are subjected. As the young men in Awarta discussing their criteria for marriage may have felt regarding their own individual and communal identity, Hammami has explained that marriages based on common community and kinship links are a way of preserving the continued identity of diaspora communities.[11] Such may also be the case in communities that have suffered the effects of isolation, in which kin relations have become so important. The constant threat that the village itself may disappear as a result of the expansion of and violent aggression from Itamar settlement, as well as the disappearance of economic life in the village due to years of siege, restrictions on agricultural cultivation and neglect by the PA,[12] creates an atmosphere in which the community does appear to be under a very real threat, and thus such ties within the community and family become all the more important.

The politicization of the Covid-19 pandemic in 2020 also caused drastic disruptions in the social relations of Palestinians. Border closures imposed by both Israel and the PA exacerbated the already-fragile economic situation of the population living from day-to-day as well as reducing the presences of internationals in Palestinian areas during a time when settlement expansion was increasing. High infection rates in Palestinian communities also led to more people self-isolating as well as isolating their elderly family members. The isolation of elderly has had profound effects on their psychological well-being as well as local social life as family interaction is not only a foundation of society but in the Palestinian context often the only reliable structure for maintaining a sense of normalcy in everyday life.

Because of the long-term siege on Nablus and the physical division of the villages around it, territorial and social borders have been hardened between these communities, making the cultural relationship to place central within the individual communities. In the worlds constructed within various Palestinian communities everyday life may differ drastically due to those communities' physical, political and social isolation from each other. These social divisions are the results of the imposed isolation of the communities but also a cause of the continued social fragmentation, in that they perpetuate themselves in the perceptions of the population. Through the experience of prolonged isolation, different conceptions of local identity have developed and are emphasized across various segments of society. The experiences of daily life in rural villages, refugee camps and the urban centre, even in the Nablus region alone, are not only different but the ways in which people express themselves, experience violence and make sense of their world are unique to those communities. From the perspective of the Israeli domination and the imposition of isolation throughout the second intifada in order to stifle resistance and control the Palestinian population, biopolitics can be viewed as a framework through which to view the divisions of people into different categories and social groups. Foucault defines the practice of biopolitics as being able 'to rationalize problems presented to governmental practice by the phenomena characteristic of a group of living human beings constituted as a population: health, sanitation, birth rate, longevity, race'. In this method of categorization, biopolitics is used by the modern state to hold the power over a population 'to foster life or disallow it to the point of death'.[13] Through settler-colonial domination and administration, practices of regulation, exclusion and discipline contain, control and divide the native population. Biopolitics perpetuates labelling and division, as well as the exclusion, non-recognition and elimination of Palestinian lives.[14]

Perhaps one of the most tangible and apparent examples of biopolitics in the Israeli domination over Palestinian life is the use of census data, labelling and identification documents. For Palestinians, the ID card not only determines if one can or cannot move through a checkpoint, it dictates their allocation of rights and determines their status as citizens and non-citizens. Prior to 1948, Palestinians were issued British Mandate identification defining them as 'Turkish subjects that habitually live in Palestine'. After the creation of Israel, those who came to live in the West Bank were given temporary Jordanian IDs and those in Gaza were given Egyptian. After 1967, Israel issued distinctively different forms of identification to Palestinians living in the West Bank, Gaza and East Jerusalem, these forms of ID governed who could go where and what rights they had as non-citizens. After the creation of the PA, Palestinians in the West Bank and Gaza were given orange and green PA-issued IDs granting them 'Palestinian citizenship', while those in East Jerusalem hold temporary Israeli residency permits stating that they have no citizenship. As Helga Tawil-Souri explains, 'ID cards speak directly to that cognitive dissonance with which Palestinians live: fearing that the Israeli state wants them disappeared, yet simultaneously being rendered subjects of the state's bureaucratic machine.'[15] Through the classification of people by their ethnic background and geographic location, the Israeli apparatus administers power over Palestinian life, defining what rights the individual has and what laws they are subject to. The obscuring of the individual through obligatory ID systems and the determination of their rights and worth as persons through complex and ambiguous permit systems and bureaucratic labelling reduce the person to existing as a subject of Israeli control. Through counting, differentiating, documenting and disciplining Palestinians, the occupied population has come to be subjected and controlled.

State power, according to Foucault, requires sovereignty, which must be displayed publicly and inflicted on the subordinated population,[16] meaning that in order for sovereignty to exist the relations of power must be exercised throughout the entire population. Nir Gazit uses the term 'fragmented sovereignty' to describe the way that Israel and the PA operate; as occupied territory lacks a clear border or political status, geographical space is not static but constantly changing and 'state agents' interpret and manipulate conceptions of sovereignty at their convenience in order to assert power.[17] Essentially this is to say that any notions of Palestinian sovereignty have been 'undone' in that 'the State detaches itself from direct, intense involvement and thus deinstitutionalizes and decentralizes its jurisdiction'.[18] Talal Asad elaborates on the Foucauldian critique of power, noting the 'contrast between sovereign power, which needs to be displayed publicly and disciplinary power which works through the normalisation of everyday behaviour'.[19] The normalization of occupation and isolation has led to a fracturing of conceptions of the Palestinian nation, culture and identity. Because various segments of the Palestinian population in the West Bank have been treated differently, isolated from one another and allowed different rights, they have been further removed from each other as communities not only physically but also socially. The Israeli state may arbitrarily deny a community the right to exist while at the same time easing the restrictions on another one. The PA as a state-like actor also imposes itself on the Palestinian population, rewarding some communities with a certain level of safety and affluence while allowing others, mainly rural villages and refugee camps, to descend into deeper levels of poverty.

The Palestinian panopticon

The structures of surveillance that exist in the occupied territories are complex and multifaceted. Various forms of technological surveillance monitor communications and media, and widespread paranoia exists in many communities over suspicions that they are embedded with various informants working for Israel, the PA's intelligence apparatus or a range of political movements. In the case of Nablus specifically, watch towers and military bases with series of antennas and monitoring equipment are clearly visible at any location in the city, as they outline the horizon of the mountain tops that encircle Nablus, serving as a constant physical reminder that the population lives in a panopticon. This condition of constant surveillance creates an atmosphere of paranoia that has grown significantly since the end of the second intifada, due to violent conflicts between political factions and brutal repercussions by the PA security forces on opponents of the post-Oslo status quo. A result of increased surveillance amid attempts by the PA to consolidate power in the West Bank, as well as Hamas in Gaza following 2007, has generated distrust within communities. In some cases families have become divided due to contrasting loyalties and rumours of certain people being secretly employed as informants for the PA, Hamas or Israel.

Foucault explains that the panopticon is 'a way of defining power relations in terms of the everyday life of men'.[20] According to Deleuze, panoptoconism is not about discipline but control. Discipline relies on the enclosure of social space whereas control encourages mobility in order to manage the entire population.[21] Through the use of technology, identity documents and informants the Israeli surveillance apparatus maintains a degree of control over the population of Nablus, as they are seen without being able to see. Because the public assumes that internet and telecommunications are monitored and that drones and surveillance towers surrounding the city may be recording their actions, a degree of control is imposed on them without them necessarily knowing that they are being watched. Biopolitical control, which is inflicted on the Palestinian population through the use of biometric IDs, complex obligatory permit systems, surveillance over telecommunications and paranoia in everyday life, keeps society in a state of perpetual uncertainty.

The position of the Palestinian Authority throughout the second intifada has been ambiguous, to say the least. The position of the Palestinian people regarding the PA has been a point of great contention and has contributed significantly to, if not been one of the core causes of, social fragmentation among Palestinians living under occupation. Security cooperation and coordination between the PA's security service and the Israeli military is a point of contention among the general population as the role of the PA and its relationship with the Palestinian people is often contradictory. In Nablus, the PA had very little presence in terms of security personnel during the second intifada, in part because of Israeli siege and invasions but also because much of the community did not tolerate their authority. The PA's secret police did, however, keep track of the activities of the public and especially of the various armed groups that regulated the city. One resident of Nablus's Old City recounted to me that following the schism between Fatah and Hamas in 2007, elite elements of the PA's security apparatuses were recruited to infiltrate the besieged town and assassinate rival fighters.

Following years of being unable to operate in Nablus through the second intifada as well as a growing and bitter divide with Hamas, since 2009 the Palestinian Authority's security forces have not only made significantly public appearances in the streets but have also engaged in regular anti-insurgency style raids. In Nablus, PA security forces and police are informed when the Israeli military is going to invade the city, at which point they must by regulation change into civilian clothing and stay off the streets. There have also been instances of much deeper PA and Israeli collaboration, beyond raids to arrest political opponents and resistance fighters. PA forces have also started to be involved in coordinated escorts for settlers to visit Joseph's Tomb in Nablus, protecting them from residents of nearby Balata refugee camp. Such instances have not only sent contradictory messages to the Palestinian public regarding the role of the PA but, as many residents feel, test the boundaries of what the people can be forced to accept.

Multiple levels of surveillance of the Palestinian population have become normalized over decades of occupation focusing not only on political activities but on deeply personal and existential matters. Mapping of a civilian population involves the intelligence apparatus knowing not only where people live but their specific social relations, even more intimately than members of their communities and even families. In 2014 a public letter issued by forty-three members of Israeli elite electronic intelligence unit 8,200 confirmed that surveillance aims were focused not on security but to create divisions within the society.[22] The letter details instructions to research and exploit socially damaging information on Palestinians such as sexual preferences, financial status and infidelities in order to blackmail individuals and use them as collaborators.[23] Israeli intelligence has been exposed as particularly targeting homosexual Palestinians for extortion.

The Israeli military-intelligence apparatus exerts not only knowledge and control, but power over the very existence of individuals. The systematic social breakdown of community, even down to the fracturing of the family unit, through intimidation, paranoia and engineered rivalries within communities, represents attacks on individual identity itself.

Alone in a world

The isolation and closure imposed during and beyond the second intifada have reinforced the importance of kinship structures within communities, while at the same time weakening the structures of civil society that had formerly existed.[24] However, as Johnson points out, kinship structures are also under threat due to physical and social isolation, as siege and restrictions on mobility negatively affect the mobilization of kinship networks.[25] Violence is used by both Israeli and Palestinian elements to create a layers of social exclusion and segregation that are reproduced as social divisions within Palestinian society. The conditions of control over Palestinian life in the West Bank extend far beyond military occupation, political oppression and total surveillance; the very social fabric of life within the community and even family is kept in a constant state of disorientation. Through long-term isolation and the maintenance of a state of uncertainty and distrust of others, the social life of communities is as fragmented as the land itself. This can be seen in the process by which the social organization that had been mediated through political movements has disappeared and general cohesion between communities has all but collapsed. While attempts at community revival may prove unsuccessful, simple acts of survival and resilience constitute ways in which individuals, as families and communities, try to compensate for the lack of a manageable social situation. Despite this direct fragmenting of the social structure itself, individuals and families still attempt to maintain their identity as a community.

Burin is a clear example of a disappearing village. The tiny community, which sits in a valley between two settlements and a number of small outposts, comes under daily attack. The village is under constant watch from the hilltops and under siege throughout the second intifada to the extent that no one left. Military jeeps continue to patrol the few small streets as the village remains under curfew after dark.

Fatima was a widowed woman in her late sixties living alone in Burin. She had, however, managed to maintain control over her household at the edge of the village, which bordered the bypass road leading to the entrance of Yitzhar settlement. Her children and grandchildren were generally present and helped her a great deal, though there was no question as to who was in charge. The house itself was quite small, only one floor, and had the remains of a neighbouring chicken house which had been burned down and a few scattered olive trees in front. On the safer side of the house, the one facing away from the road, Fatima often sat under grapevines she had cared for where she could enjoy the view of the village facing away from the settlement. All of her windows were perpetually boarded up and she saw no reason to replace them as stones were thrown on a nightly basis; she gestured to a collection of large stones that had been thrown by the settlers which she kept in a pile in the corner of her porch. When I spoke with her regarding isolation and the situation of the village, she noted internal problems within families and the community such as men having nothing to do and becoming angry with the women, and young people not knowing anything outside of their village. However, her strongest criticisms were towards the 'outsiders', the urban Palestinian communities of Nablus and Ramallah. Fatima asserted:

> The people in the cities have forgotten about us, the young people don't even know about us. They have no appetite for resistance, they do business with the Israelis during the day and then their homes and cars are attacked [by settlers] at night. I am left here alone with the settlers. They will finish us.

Fatima's resentment of the urban population, which she felt had not undergone the suffering of the rural people and had forgotten the villages, expresses the divide felt between the rural and urban communities. Perhaps her reaction and assertion that 'the people in the cities do business with the Israelis' was in response to the fruitless diplomatic negotiations conducted by the PA and the absence of any PA services in the Area C village. I learned some months after visiting Fatima that PA security forces had actually entered the village in order to sever the electric lines leading to a mosque near the entrance of the village, the largest and most modern structure in the in Burin, which had been constructed only to be threatened with demolition orders by the Israeli authorities, as its towering minaret was considered a security threat and annoyance by the neighbouring settlements. This level of coordination between the Israeli military and the PA security apparatus reinforces the popular belief among the population that the PA itself is a policeman for Israel. Examples of PA security coordination with Israel also contribute to an already-existing social stigma that has developed between the rural and urban areas in that the rural population feels both neglect and antagonism from the Palestinian elite.

The radical individualism in the urban youth that Fatima referred to is a concern that has been expressed by many residents living in marginalized communities. Having grown up during the second intifada and witnessed the displays of absolute power by the Israeli military have created a fear that urban youth are willing to accept conditions of a 'contained normalcy' within the enclaves of Area A. For the rural population residing in Area C, this is not an option and in many cases a level of resentment has developed in those who feel that the larger Palestinian community has abandoned them. Such circumstances reflect the conditions that occur in a variety of post-colonial examples. Through the uses of ethnic and class stratification as well as the creation of docile colonized elite, former colonial powers and their local agents continue to maintain control over indigenous societies to serve their interests. Dividing the public, creating class differences and isolating communities all create a situation of radical individualism in which the resistance that had previously united the population is ignored, as Bourdieu eloquently illustrates:

> To tear oneself from the world in order to confront or master it is to tear oneself from the immediate present and the immediate 'forthcoming', an urgency and threat with which the present is fraught. The sub-proletarian, locked in the present, knows only the free-floating indefinite future of his daydreams. Because the field of possibilities has the same limits as the field of objective possibilities, the individual project and the revolutionary consciousness are closely allied.[26]

Paranoia and uncertainty of life

Increasingly since 2010 residents of Nablus have reported raids and arrest in villages and refugee camps conducted by the PA security forces, targeting not only militants and politically critical figures but also community leaders. People have expressed the opinion that the actions of the PA are not only forcibly smothering any opposition but also preventing any potential resistance to possible Israeli aggression. Such actions are viewed by much of the Nablus population as destroying any opportunities for small communities to function in any alternative frameworks to the ones that have sustained their poverty. Increasingly, cooperation between the PA and Israel has resulted in widespread paranoia among the Palestinian population. In the same period, the PA has also moved to privatize much of the civil infrastructure, such as electricity and water, in the areas for which it is responsible. These developments have led to a growing paranoia among some Palestinians in Nablus that the PA will be reformed into a network of small municipal governments inside the Palestinian urban enclaves, while all of Area C and the Palestinian villages inside them might be officially annexed by Israel.

What the future of a Palestinian government or state might look like and the possibility that Area C may be annexed by Israel are difficult to speculate about, and while they exist as very real fears in the minds of many of them, Palestinians are helpless to change their situations or imagine their futures with any degree of certainty. In the everyday lives of the people living in Nablus-area villages, what is relevant is the fear that the population expresses of not knowing what is going on and not knowing what will happen next. For many, this is expressed as a fear of being erased, of finally being 'disappeared' by the Israeli entity. For Fatima in Burin and for the young men in Awarta, such fears speak to the realities of their everyday lives. Everyday life in Burin and Awarta consists of experiences of violence, uncertainty and boredom. The rather profound response of the young men in Awarta to my enquiry about marriage that their families would cease to continue if they did not marry and have children within their community speaks to both the very real fear of extinction that all Palestinians to some degree feel, and the tight bonds between kin and community that manifest when the future of the society is under threat. In the case of Burin, the village has all but disappeared. While a little more than a thousand people reside there, they are almost constantly losing land and homes, the youth have few, if any, prospects in the village, yet the village is all that they have ever known.

Disorientation and identity

The social fragmentation of Palestinian society has occurred on many levels from the physical barriers created by the occupation itself to what much of the population perceives to be the ulterior motives of the Palestinian elite to maintain a certain status quo. Distrust of the leadership and pseudo-governing body as well as distrust between individuals in communities severs the solidarity of the first intifada, which is often idealistically invoked. There exist many complex dynamics that foster the social inclusion of certain segments of Palestinian society and the exclusion of others and that have manifested themselves in a variety of ways in different communities. Through variations in the treatment of different communities, and the isolation of the communities themselves from one another, the social divisions between them have grown significantly. Violence has been effectively used as a tool to control, unite and divide the Palestinian people for more than seventy-five years, and it has come to define the Palestinian experience culturally for both those in diaspora and those under occupation. Taussig discusses the use of prolonged disorder through acts of violence as maintaining a situation of 'terror as usual' in order to disorient the public and gain control.[27] Terror, as Taussig argues, is what keeps the population in a position that maintains the normality of the situation created by the perpetual 'state of emergency'.[28]

Labels such as colonialism and apartheid have been used to describe the social conditions in the occupied West Bank, and while elements of all of these exist, none fully define the situation of fragmentation on a social level. The divisions created in the West Bank since the second intifada have resulted in what have become different Palestinian societies, the rural and the urban, living parallel to one another. Years of geographical and political isolation have led to a situation of collective anomie in which people from different communities have had completely different life experiences and are not able to relate to each other. Through this fragmentation of Palestinian society itself and the reinforcement of a situation of limbo, the possibility of genuine organized resistance is diminished and the population remains focused on their division. Bourdieu has described the inability of marginalized Algerians to change their situation as a result of their social circumstances.

> Because poverty imposes itself on them with a necessity so total that is allows them no glimpse of a reasonable exit, sub-proletarians tend to live their suffering as habitual and even natural, as an inevitable ingredient in their existence; and because they do not passes the indispensable minimum of security and culture, they cannot clearly conceive the total change in the social order which could abolish the cause of their suffering.[29]

The apparatus of control over Palestinian lives in the West Bank has gone beyond simply allowing or denying individuals the right to live. It has disoriented the public to degree that they can no longer collectively conceptualize the Palestinian nation. Aspects of collective consciousness, as intimate as culture and identity, have become incoherent and cannot be articulated in the same ways by urban and rural West Bank residents. Many Palestinians reminisce about the first intifada as a time when the people, regardless of social stratification, united in a common cause.

Regardless of whether this unification of the population was as genuine as it is remembered to have been or if it is to some degree the idealization of an imagined past,[30] the mobilization that occurred did profoundly shape Palestinian society and defined certain common goals that remain in the social memory. The deterioration in the social power of political parties following a shift from mass mobilization to development after the creation of the PA, and the tendency to revert to local forms of social organization following the failure of Oslo and the second intifada, have allowed the perpetuation of social divisions between Palestinian communities beyond the physical divisions imposed by the Israeli military. Through the creation of elite segments of Palestinian society that can exert control over and marginalize others, unprecedented social stratification has been created. Throughout the second intifada, the people of Nablus have lived their lives trapped in their isolated worlds.

The severing of the communities from one another and various levels of isolation imposed over time has led to a situation in which Palestinians have drastically different experiences of everyday life depending on the location they may find themselves in. While divisions between communities have been increasingly imposed, the processes of social fragmentation themselves have over time also had a paradoxically unifying effect. Displays of solidarity with West Bank villages under threat by settlements, residents of East Jerusalem at risk of displacement and Palestinians in Gaza living under siege and bombardment, have become common across all segments of Palestinian society, including refugees in diaspora and Arab citizens of Israel. A generation of Palestinians that have grown up since the second intifada and largely isolated within their segments of society has rejected old political discourses and the rhetoric of political leaders. What is characteristic about more recent social movements and mobilization across Palestinian society is that it is rooted in local movements and managed within communities, and, unlike the intifadas before, rejects the presence of political parties and is largely without leadership. To this extent the same long-term divisions which have led to the fragmentation of Palestine are also creating a common unity through shared frustrations.

Figure 3 Palestinian civil defence volunteers. Maroof Rabba' leads a group of emergency medical volunteers during a rescue operation. Photo by author.

5

Development, divisions and debt

This chapter offers a brief overview of the relationships between the PA, NGOs and international aid as they have impacted social structure in Palestinian communities. Throughout the second intifada the diverse neighbourhoods and villages in Nablus have been treated in drastically different ways, not only by the occupying Israeli power but by the PA and the international community as well. I argue that because certain segments of Palestinian society have received international support and others have been excluded, differences and a contentious relationship between various Palestinian communities have been created and have contributed to the social division of the Palestinian people. This chapter will examine the social implications of international aid and look at the NGO and aid industry that has developed in Palestine. International NGOs not only provide services to communities, they also alter the social relations of the communities in which they operate. The international community's influence on the Palestinian economy and the structure of the PA has had significant effects on how communities functioned throughout the second intifada and how they have become divided. With foreign countries funding the PA to regulate security and NGOs to provide services to the Palestinian population in the West Bank, specific economic interests have been promoted and the concept of 'Palestine' as an economy without a state has been at least partially absorbed into a neoliberal paradigm, the results of which will be explored in this chapter.

Social implications of international aid in Palestine

To a large degree much of the resilience displayed in Palestinian society shortly after the Israeli occupation of the West Bank and Gaza was emphasized in voluntary work groups organized by student movements in the 1970s.[1] At the time these movements were facilitated by the PFLP, DFLP and the Communist Party in order to assist farmers affected by the mass migration of workers to Israel in what Tamari describes as a 'coherent retrieve[al of] the land ideology […] with echoes of 19th century Russian Narodnism'.[2] Widespread ideological efforts and examples of solidarity on such a scale have not been seen in Palestine since the first intifada. With the creation of the Palestinian Authority and the opening of the floodgates for international aid, many services are now provided by international NGOs, which in many cases make it seemingly unproductive for Palestinians to pursue organic community development. Palestinians have instead been encouraged to pursue self-interest and the accumulation of wealth in order to become something of a middle class, at the expense of seeking to maintain stability in their communities. More recent efforts to produce 'economic peace' in the West Bank by offering microloans to Palestinians and encouraging spending and investment in the urban areas are now proving to have disastrous consequences.

While Nablus area villages had historically been fairly self-sufficient in terms of sustaining their populations on what they produced through agriculture, as communities they faced many adverse changes following the Israeli occupation in 1967. Many Palestinians living in diaspora, as well as others from West Bank villages, took opportunities to work as labour in the oil-producing Gulf States in order to send money back to their communities. In addition to direct support from family members working abroad, the PLO taxed all diaspora Palestinians 5 per cent of their wages, much of which was sent to maintain the populations living in occupied Palestinian villages as steadfast funds. Following the Gulf War in 1991, hundreds of thousands of diaspora Palestinians working as labour in the Gulf were expelled as a result of the PLO's decision to support Saddam Hussein. The sudden absence of steadfast funds in Palestinian villages in addition to the closing of the Israeli labour market to Palestinian workers, which had been available to them since 1967, resulted in rural villages being plunged into greater degrees of poverty. This sudden change resulted in a radical economic disparity between rural and urban Palestinian communities, given other changes taking place in the early 1990s such as the marginalization of the leftist movements which had been active in villages due to the fall of the Soviet Union, the creation of the PA and greater investment in building up the urban centres of Area A.

The Oslo Accords signed in 1993 were intended to build peace in the context of the Western concept of a two-state solution consisting of Israel and an independent Palestine. The idea behind the Oslo Accords was that there would be a five-year period of internationally brokered and funded peace building initiatives that would result in the establishment of a stable Palestinian state. Helga Tawil-Souri has noted that 'development projects are plentiful in the territories, they have not resulted in successful state-, nation- or peace building, but have marginalized indigenous civic institutions and further impoverished the Palestinian population by maintaining Israeli economic dominance over Palestinian life'.[3] It has been argued that Oslo set up the framework for the PA as a client to Israel and the international donor community.[4] The PA has long been perceived by a great deal of the Palestinian population as a watchdog for Israel, the frustration with which contributed to the outbreak of the second intifada.

Following the Oslo Accords, the international community, particularly the European Union and the United States, committed substantial development aid to the newly formed Palestinian Authority. Between 1994 and mid-2002 the international community committed almost US$65 billion to the PA, representing one of the largest examples of development aid in the world.[5] The agendas for Palestinian development were designed by various coordinating committees operated by the United Nations and the World Bank, which also controlled the flow of international aid to the PA.[6]

The economic implications in societies where 'peace building' initiatives are carried out have far-reaching effects not only in terms of providing such items as food and humanitarian assistance but also in connection with establishing relationships between local and external actors, often changing the dynamics of local social structures and elite hierarchies in the process. As was the case in past colonial projects, post-colonial interactions between the 'developed' and 'undeveloped' worlds generally take place through the conduit of local elites in societies in which external actors, former colonial or neoliberal powers, have interest. 'Peace building' aid in the Palestinian context, as Brynen notes, is about politics rather than the developmental needs of the people in that its aim is about restructuring internal power relations in order to suit donors' interests.[7]

The economic situation of the West Bank Palestinian population has been shaped and restructured by the international community. Historically an agrarian peasant society, networks and means of employment have been changed by access to the Israeli labour market, and the development of the Palestinian Authority. The creation of the PA in 1993 both legitimized international investment in a future Palestinian state and relieved Israel of the responsibility under the Fourth Geneva Convention for providing basic services and infrastructure to the populating living under its continued military occupation. Methods of income generation in the West Bank have largely changed from agriculture to construction and manual labour in Israel and to bureaucratic and service sector jobs through the PA. Currently the vast majority of all salaries in the West Bank are paid by international aid distributed through the PA. Given the uncertain status of the PA and its current economic dependency on foreign aid, not to mention the uncertainty about whether it will even exist in the not so distant future, income in the West Bank is unpredictable.

The PA government and other Palestinian institutions, including universities, are dependent on international aid, and little has been done in the post-Oslo period in terms of developing alternative and innovative methods for self-sufficiency and generating incomes from within the Palestinian population. The absence of such alternatives and emphasis on donor funding has created a society in which virtually all institutions are dependent on grants, loans and donations. NGOs dependent on donor aid have replaced the grassroots development that emerged in the 1980s prior to the establishment of the PA, which has contributed to demobilizing the population and fragmenting the nationalist unity along with it.

Changes in NGOs and community relations

During the 1980s, in the lead-up to the first intifada, a network and infrastructure of organizations was fully developed, which had a popular base within individual communities and was able to effectively provide basic services to the population. These grassroots organizations were also able to lead the Palestinian masses in direct confrontation with the occupier.[8] Following the signing of the Oslo Accords as well as the fall of the Soviet Union, international involvement in the Palestinian cause changed profoundly and under the new arrangements international development aid relived Israel of any legal obligation as an occupying power to provide civil services to the Palestinian population. The newly formed Palestinian Authority was structured as an entity dependent on Western aid based on a neoliberal model. Sari Hanafi and Linda Tabar have described the shift in the political economy of aid to NGOs in Palestine as having

> created new internal forms of social and political capital, as well as new forms of exclusion. It is essential to recognize that the availability of new forms of bilateral and multilateral assistance to NGOs induced a state of competition between Palestinian organizations. This resulted in a struggle for organizational survival between the urban middle class activists in the NGOs and the traditional elite in the charitable societies and grassroots leadership within the committees.[9]

Before the formation of the PA, Palestinian society was organized around grassroots organizations and NGOs which were linked to political parties. NGOs provided health care, education, agricultural relief and many other services to the population.[10] After the creation of the PA, many individuals who had been prominent activists during the first intifada became leaders of service-providing NGOs, effecting what Hammami has described as a transformation from grassroots civic organizations to a professionalized elite.[11] Because of the transformation from political mass mobilization to developmental institutions, NGOs faced drastic changes from grassroots activism to organizations with an increasing upward accountability to their donors.[12] Because of the new relations of power between the PA, the international donor community and former political activists working in NGOs, many disputes developed between the PA and NGOs, which viewed themselves as representing civil society. Following the Oslo Accords, international donors were no longer able to fund Palestinian NGOs directly and instead had to fund the PA which distributed funds to NGOs. In 1995, soon after its formation, the PA attempted to pass a draft NGO law, as is common in other Arab countries, restricting the operations of NGOs in order to control the flow of money to them through a trust fund and regulate against NGOs which did not serve the PA's political agendas.[13] Because Palestinian NGOs had a long history of existing primarily as grassroots movements free to operate and seek funding in the absence of the state, many of them were well connected and well organized, and they were thus able to pressure the PA to form a more liberal NGO law, which was instituted in 2000.[14] The relationship between the PA and Palestinian NGOs has continued to be contentious; the PA still regulates funding and dictates which NGOs are allowed to operate, often based on political affiliations and personal connections. The most fundamental transformation of NGOs from before and after the creation of the PA is that they are now viewed more as political structures that are both dependent on the PA and in some cases working against its authoritarian behaviour.[15] Palestinian NGOs have a complicated relationship with both the PA and the public. While they are reliant on the flow of international funding, which is filtered through the PA, many NGOs build closer relationships with much of the population as they are the ones disbursing aid at the local level.

Former activists who have become leaders and directors of NGOs, as well as other Palestinians with connections to international organizations, have come to represent a new class of elite.[16] Describing the civil society organization that existed prior to the emergence of the PA, Rema Hammami has noted that Palestine was the only place in the Middle East where it would have been possible to create a 'strong pluralistic infrastructure of NGOs'.[17] The absence of an indigenous government combined with the grassroots initiatives and popular committees that held communities together offered the potential for creating a highly democratic governmental apparatus.[18] As the PA was formed, many of the activists who had previously been involved in political factions formed NGOs for various reasons; many leftists viewed NGOs as an alternative to the PA while others viewed them as potential mobilizers of popular resistance.[19]

As part of the Oslo process, the PA adopted neoliberal economic free-trade policies based on agreements with the International Monetary Fund (IMF) and World Bank. Because of obligations to the donor community, funding administered by the World Bank and political motivations of the PA, many large NGOs fell into the neoliberal paradigm that shaped the post-Oslo power relations in the Occupied Territories. Palestinians employed by NGOs enjoy a higher salary than those working in the mid to lower range in the PA bureaucracy,[20] as well as privileges in status, and in many cases they are allowed physical movement not extended to normal Palestinians, making employment with NGOs among the most lucrative prospects available to Palestinians.

As political parties have lost their influence in communities and popular emphasis has shifted from political mobilization to development, international NGOs have appeared and as such have altered the dynamics of communities in which they work. In terms of providing basic services to the population, small Palestinian NGOs, many of which emerged from the grassroots framework of the first intifada, offer agricultural relief, set up small medical clinics and provide other forms of very basic assistance in a wide range of communities, while there is a tendency for the large international NGOs to invest in cities, although foreign governments may fund small projects such as school construction in rural areas. Through the distribution of international funds NGOs create new elites within communities and put people related to them at an advantage. Corruption among both Palestinians and internationals in the aid community is common, if not expected, and as one informant put it:

> even if a well-meaning Palestinian is put in charge of a project, they will be forced to pay bribes to PA officials or other powerful members of the community, otherwise they will not be allowed to exist. But if only internationals are in charge then they will have no relationship or connection to the people who are supposed to be the beneficiaries and will either not care or not understand when corruption is taking place.

Helga Tawil-Souri notes the contradictions of many international projects in Palestine, particularly USAID-funded projects:

> New hierarchies have emerged where grassroots and oppositional movements are no longer funded […] western NGOs and USAID contribute to the status quo. As such, they do not engage with Palestinian society nor respond to Palestinian society's needs, but construct and dictate new needs. Moreover, the marginalization that results creates animosity and tension between the grassroots movements and westernized or western NGOs, as well as between the latter and Palestinian society.[21]

Between 2006 and 2009 USAID built a series of roads to the south and east of Nablus to connect several villages which had become cut off by settlements; however, the roads have since remained closed to Palestinian traffic due to security reasons. However, although the roads exist, they have remained closed to Palestinian residents for security reasons. In other parts of the West Bank USAID has funded road construction to replace those turned into settler

80   *The Fragmentation of Palestine*

bypass highways. The construction of these roads does not merely serve to help Palestinians get around but justifies them not using Israeli-only roads. This type of development only serves to further segregate the Palestinian population from the growing population of Israeli settlers. Tawil-Souri elaborates:

> USAID programmes need to be understood in terms of what they do not support. For example, one sector that could generate growth and a sustainable economy as opposed to creating an IT centre or a technology incubator is agriculture. However, farming and agriculture require ownership of, if not at least access to land a move that Israel opposes.[22]

Aside from corruption and counterproductive policies, many well-meaning NGOs simply cannot exist in the Occupied Territories without the permission of the Israeli authorities and therefore have no choice but to be compliant with the restrictions imposed upon them. In his article on VIP privileges for NGO workers in exchange for silence on political issues, Jeremy Wildeman argues that Israel tightly regulates the abilities of international NGOs to work in the Occupied Territories. International NGOs that operate in the West Bank and Gaza in order to provide basic services to the Palestinian population are dependent on Israeli approval of their activities in order to maintain their access to the territories. According to Wildeman, if an international NGO – or any of its workers – expresses advocacy or political sympathy for Palestinians, it risks being shut down.[23]

Local perceptions of international aid

There are hundreds of small local and international NGOs operating in Palestine and, particularly since 2009, many in Nablus as well. The general perception of NGOs and other aid organizations in Nablus is that, while they are physically present in the community, they are powerful entities with large sums of money and, more importantly, international connections and should not necessarily be trusted. NGOs, particularly international ones, establish their presence in Palestine by building offices in gated buildings and tend to maintain a somewhat exclusive atmosphere. Many internationals working in Palestinian NGOs tend to shield themselves behind institutional walls, avoiding contact with locals, while local Palestinians who work for NGOs develop an elite status in the community, not only in terms of having a higher salary than their peers and in some cases being given special permissions which might ease their personal experience of occupation, but also in terms of local community structure. Years of siege and isolation of the various neighbourhoods and villages that make up Nablus have resulted in these communities becoming increasingly tightly knit. The increasing presence of international NGOs within the communities has produced more changes than simply altering the dynamics of services and aid. While some level of curiosity surrounds international organizations based in Nablus, there is also a high degree of animosity, as it is not made clear to a majority of locals what these organizations are actually doing and if they are in fact contributing anything to the community. Many Palestinians working for NGOs and international organizations face social stigma in their communities both as a result of their unique privilege and because of resentment arising from a sense of betrayal of an obligation to the community.

During the post-Oslo period, the PA adopted neoliberal economic free-trade policies. Such policies were a result of donor interventions, particularly the PA's agreements with the IMF and World Bank as well as USAID. Some results of the PA's and international community's implementation of neoliberal policies in the West Bank have inhibited the Palestinian private sector and in many ways hindered economic development at a local level. In addition to the effects of the occupation on the Palestinian economy, the PA's approach of favouring foreign investment as opposed to organic development has had adverse effects on rural areas. In villages near settlements such as Awarta and Burin, it has been made easier for villagers to acquire food aid and cheaper for them to rely on imports than it is for them to farm their land. Palestinian farmers and producers are unable to compete with the availability of cheaper imported products that flood the markets, as a result of which they cannot produce effectively and the population cannot afford local goods. On an agricultural level, USAID and other international donors have focused on enterprise development as opposed to promoting sustainability by setting up programmes for farmers to grow flowers and cash crops for export. Palestinian produce that meets international standards is exported through private agribusiness companies that provide the farmer with a slight increase in income, while low-quality Israeli produce is placed in the Palestinian market.[24] Such policies contribute directly to the growing rates of poverty and food insecurity in Palestinian communities.

Both the PA and the aid industry benefit from the current configuration of the aid economy in the West Bank, regardless of whether the aid-funded projects accomplish any of their stated goals or offer any benefit to the Palestinian population. Many small NGOs, and especially large funders such as USAID and the Japanese International Cooperation Agency (JICA), spend the majority of aid on funding local and international contractors and consultants, leaving only a small portion of donor funding to be spent on actual aid projects.[25] The former PA agriculture minister actually went as far as to publicly criticize JICA after it became apparent that only US$700,000 of a US$6 million aid project had been used for its intended purposes over the three-year duration of the project.[26] According to a 2008 USAID-funded report, out of the hundreds of NGOs in the West Bank most of them were inactive or did not implement regular programmes. In Nablus area villages, 80 per cent of service activities are provided through Hamas-affiliated NGOs, including healthcare and kindergarten facilities.[27] While more than 50 per cent of NGOs in Nablus are international or Fatah-affiliated, many of them are inactive or support the individual needs of elites.[28]

The organization Global Communities (formally known as CHF International) is a major subcontractor of USAID projects in the Palestinian territories. CHF runs food security programmes and community assistance programmes aimed at improving basic infrastructure in the most impoverished communities. However, as was explained to me by a CHF employee, the main task of CHF is thoroughly vetting any potential beneficiary of USAID-funded programmes, including children. CHF conducts intensive background checks on Palestinians applying to take part in USAID-funded programmes in order to exclude those deemed to be security risks, as well as their family members, which includes anyone with connections to Hamas or other Islamist groups or anyone who has at any time been arrested by the Israeli military or the PA. Restrictions on receiving international aid have been placed not only on individuals and their families but entire communities are in some cases blacklisted from certain aid projects as a result of community member's support for Hamas or activities deemed damaging by USAID's protocols. The systematic exclusion that is built into the international aid process is intrinsic to shaping the future of Palestinian society in the neoliberal paradigm that has been adopted by the international community and the PA. Through offering opportunities and aid to certain segments of society while excluding others, the international community alters the dynamics of Palestinian communities while also contributing to their social fragmentation.

Ambiguities of power in local organizations

The second intifada was in many ways as much of a display of frustration with the PA and Palestinian elite as it was with the ongoing Israeli occupation. Residents in Nablus recount the years of siege during the second intifada not only in the destruction from Israeli airstrikes and trauma of invasions, but also in the chaos wrought by gangs and criminality. The fighters who defended Nablus during the many invasions are remembered in romantic and heroic imagery, and many charismatic fighters and community leaders did indeed provide much-needed cohesion in the community and even bridged political divides. But the role of armed resistance during this period is also recalled with a complicated mix of romanization and resentment. During the eight-year siege of Nablus, police and other civil institutions collapsed or were driven underground. As conditions in the city deteriorated, various elements of resistance groups mixed with criminal gangs turned to extortion and intimidation of the local community.

Although many of the men who engaged in mafia-like activities were not politically aligned, and those had been more than often serving their own interests, some belonged to various political factions including the Fatah-aligned al-Aqsa Martyrs' Brigades, which had been given birth in Balata refugee camp. Violent encounters and shootouts between groups had become common during the siege, although often results of personal rivalries as opposed to politics. Following the Battle of Gaza when Hamas took control of the Gaza Strip in June 2007, intense battles between al-Aqsa Brigade fighters and Hamas supporters erupted throughout Nablus, where Hamas had come to enjoy a large support base. Once the siege on Nablus was eased after 2009 and PA had re-established its presence in Nablus, suspected members of Hamas were frequently arrested and often brutally tortured. The suppression of Hamas supports contrasted with the reality that many Fatah-aligned fighters who had engaged in criminality during the second intifada went unpunished,[29] causing resentment among much of the community, and further marginalizing residents of the refugee camps in Nablus. The violent political schism between the PA and Hamas transcended deeper than dividing popular elements in the municipality, and extended to restructuring the ways that the general population needed to interact and communicate with one another.

Alaa took a position as director for a Palestinian NGO in Nablus in 2005. Formerly a Leftist activist, Alaa was forced to obscure his political persuasions and loyalties after he came to accumulate a great deal of social agency in the community. What had initially been a small organization of international and local activists providing aid in Nablus through the heaviest periods of fighting during the second intifada was turned into an instrument of public relations for Nablus as well as a means to bring money into the city. Alaa's ability to market to liberal Europeans and North Americans was extremely successful and, particularly after 2009, the NGO enjoyed a consistent turnover of foreign donors and volunteers bringing their own money into the organization and with a range of motivations for wanting to visit Palestine. As the organization grew, it also gained the attention of various power structures in the city, each with their own ambitions.

Alaa came from a prominent family in his village. Having studied in university abroad and fluently speaking several languages, he had a distinct advantage in Nablusi society as he had both enough local connections and international experience that he could travel with comparative ease to other Palestinians. As Alaa's influence in Nablus grew, he developed close ties with prominent figures in the PA administration as well as elements in the municipality who were ties to Hamas. As local sentiment in Nablus was largely distrusting and resentful of the PA and official institutions by the end of the second intifada; yet, any organization operating necessarily had to coordinate with both local and official actors, managing an international organization while maintaining positive public relations became an increasingly difficult balance in the besieged city. Suspicions from both the PA and the Islamist elements in the municipality regarding the loyalties of various institutions in Nablus, particularly those dealing with foreigners, were high. As a result,

Development, Divisions and Debt

operatives of both of various political movements began to keep a close watch on the NGO. This was both to keep an eye on what the foreigners were doing in the community and to keep track of how much money was being brought into Nablus and who payments were being made to.

Alaa, who had been a committed Marxist, returned to Palestine after studying in Europe with the hope of helping to build cohesion and improve resources and resilience of the community, only to find himself trapped between the authoritarian structure of the PA and the more conservative elements of Nablusi society. When Alaa first took on the role of director of what was at the time a very small organization, he had hoped to use his networking skills to acquire resources from international outreach in order to help address the immediate needs of the community during the second intifada. Many of his initiatives were quite successful, especially in the Old City and the refugee camps. Given the success of his outreach and his rapid rise to being an influential figure in Nablus, after the intifada came to an end he was able to recruit a wide range of foreign volunteers and investment. While Alaa had gained influence in Nablus he also fell into the complicated situation of having to please various opposing elements of the society. This was particularly difficult in a community that had been closed off for so long and where those with foreign ties were viewed with a great deal of suspicion. As is the case with many small NGOs and civil organizations, Alaa became caught in a precarious balancing act of having to maintain multiple loyalties in a society in which power relations are potentially shifting and uncertain.

As this example shows, international NGOs operating in Palestine are subject to regulation by various political entities both inside and outside of Palestine, as well as having to maintain an often complex relationship with the local community. The development industry funded by international donors that has manifested in Palestine has been an important component in conditioning Palestinian society to become physically and economically dependent on the international community. This to a large degree has depoliticized Palestinian society and pushed young urban Palestinians in particular to support neoliberal hegemony, which only serves to isolate the population further.[30] Palestinians working in the international aid industry constitute a new urban elite that Hanafi and Tabari argue create 'new social formations which disrupts the embeddedness of local organizations within local social networks, concomitant with the rise of the neoliberal paradigm which transforms the relationship between the individual and social institutions'.[31]

Promoting an imagined economy

The Oslo Accords not only enabled the geographic division of the West Bank and the subsequent isolation of Palestinian communities but also imposed economic isolation through the regulation of Palestinian business. In this sense the Israeli occupation is as much about control over capitalism as it is about military occupation of the land. Because Palestinian banking and tax systems are routed through Israeli institutions and all imports and exports by Palestinian businesses must go through a complicated permit system, it is difficult for Palestinians to sustain an economy. Moreover, the physical siege of Palestinian cities hinders the continued circulation of capital. Harvey notes that 'the geographical mobilities of both capital and labour power depend on the creation of fixed and immobile infrastructure'.[32] Through the geographic fragmentation of Palestinian communities the ability of the population to maintain infrastructure and economic activity is suppressed.

Throughout the history of occupation and colonialism, economic incentives for cooperation have been used as effective means of pacifying the Palestinian population. Collaboration between Palestinian leaderships and the Israeli colonial structure can be seen as early as the 1970s in such examples as Moshe Dayan's policy of open bridges and cooptation of traditional elites, and Menahem Milson's Israeli Civil Administration and Palestinian Village Leagues in the 1980s.[33] The attempts at economic improvement by the appointed PA prime minister and former IMF official Salam Fayyad have resulted in 80 per cent of the PA employees in the West Bank having debt, thanks to micro-loans which were made available as part of a plan to create 'economic peace' by temporarily stimulating the economies of West Bank cities.[34] In Nablus many people in their twenties and thirties have taken advantage of the availability of loans since 2009, in many cases to invest in training courses in order to improve their futures such as business, marketing and IT classes offered by AMIDEAST.[35] Despite heavy investment in new businesses, the availability of loans has not increased the number of employment opportunities or quality of life in Nablus.

While unemployment is extremely high in Palestine in general, the Nablus area is particularly affected due to the systematic closure of communities and difficulties in movement. In villages south of Nablus the only employment consists of few small individually owned manufacturing businesses, as in Biet Furik, and small shops with very limited items that only service the immediate community. The vast majority of residents are unemployed and those who are able to find work do so only by relocating to the urban centres of Nablus and Ramallah. The majority of those who are employed in the West Bank work in some capacity or another for the PA, which is dependent on donor funding and also dependent on Israel to allow the flow of funding to the PA to continue. It is not uncommon for public sector workers on PA-funded salaries to go two months or more without any payment. A hospital worker in Rafidia hospital in Nablus gave me an example; he was lucky to be paid 60 per cent of his salary during a month. He noted that most of his colleagues had loans to pay which amounted to 50 per cent of their salaries, so in reality they would only have 10 per cent of what they should be earning to live on for the month. He went on to tell me that in 2011, after delaying public employee salaries for three months, the PA government paid half of one month's salary prior to the start of Ramadan. This amount averaged at 1,500 NIS, as most mid-level public employees earn about 3,000 NIS per month, although after loan deductions this left the majority of employees with only 500 NIS for the month of Ramadan.

Loans have been made especially easily accessible for lower-level employees of the PA. Payments for the loans are deducted directly from the employee's salaries by the banks, which can cause unexpected complications considering that the amount that people are paid fluctuates on a monthly basis with no warning. In order for an individual working in any field of service such as health, education or the security forces to take out a loan they must have two other employees co-sign the loan agreement, so that if that individual fails to pay the loan the due amount will automatically be taken from the co-signees. The highest percentage of Palestinians took out loans between 2009 and 2011. During this time it became common in Nablus for family members and colleagues belonging to the same bank to take out loans in groups, co-signing for each other, the result being that each person would be responsible for paying back not only their own loan but the loans of two other people as well.

In *Algeria 1960* Bourdieu explains the notion of 'credit' to be the most effective tool of the colonial power in asserting economic control over the colonized society.[36] He argues that the situation of economic dependence is imposed by the imperialist power while allowing the impression that it is in accordance with the autonomous evolution of the colonized society.[37] Fayyad's economic reforms in the West Bank were sponsored largely by the United States and EU, in exchange for donations and loans of billions of dollars with the intention of stimulating the economy in select urban centres. Jeff Halper, an anthropologist and director of the Israeli Committee against House Demolitions (ICAHD), has described Fayyad's economic peace plan as 'a viable apartheid', in that Fayyad has rejected earlier demands to Israel for physical territory and instead bargained for economic space. By introducing neoliberal reforms supported by Israel, Fayyad created a situation in which the Palestinian business class could operate in a limited capacity and move their goods in the Arab world and Israeli market, with the intention that there would eventually be a trickle-down effect to the working class.[38]

The availability of credit and loans following years of siege, violence and isolation provided many a material way to compensate for the sense of helplessness imposed by occupation. This is especially evident in a spending and building boom that occurred after loans became widely available in Palestinian cities. Many middle-class Palestinians in Nablus engaged in construction projects in 2010 to build new homes or additions to existing ones, making symbolic fortresses of their homes in order to compensate for their lack of freedom. For many the fortification of the body, home or automobile creates a sense of safety in a world of uncertainty. This mentality of materialistic compensation is both financially harmful and destructive to the social solidarity of the community. With the availability of loans this type of behaviour increased dramatically, not only in terms of buying unnecessary items such as cars and large homes but also in terms of leasing store fronts in the many new buildings erected in the 'rejuvenated' city centre. After 2009 many Nablus residents had gone into tremendous debt by engaging in business activities that more often than not failed in the restricted and occupied economy. Nevertheless many USAID-funded programmes actively encourage young Palestinians to go into business and marketing in order to stimulate their own economy and gain opportunities.

The mentality shift that accompanied the replacing of liberation ideology with institution building has resulted in increased class disparity among the occupied Palestinian population. This shift was a result of the drastic economic and political changes that occurred with the creation of the PA and the internationalization of aid and development in Palestine. While many Palestinians were provided with opportunities to work in the development sector and to travel to Europe and North America for higher education, individuals living in communities that had been excluded from development programmes, for either geographic or political reasons, had been further marginalized. Further individualization, particularly among youth in the more privileged urban community, has contributed to the growing division between rural and urban communities and the social fragmentation of Palestinian society.

International cooperation and settler colonialism

Paradoxically, in an area with billions of dollars of development investment and hundreds of service-providing organizations, unemployment and poverty among Palestinians have increased since the Oslo period. Prior to the formation of the PA, NGOs were open access mass organizations with public agendas and the ability to mobilize the population. NGOs that emerged after Oslo have been dependent on foreign funding, predominantly operated by an urban elite, and more active in cities than in rural areas.[39] As community-based organizations have been replaced by larger international NGOs, communication and relationships between the service providers and the population have diminished. International aid agencies have made changes in the dynamics and social structures of the communities in which they operate through creating new elites and in some cases increasing the isolation of communities through their programmes. While NGOs are necessary for providing services to Palestinian communities, they also relieve Israel of its responsibility as an occupying power to provide basic services for the Palestinian population. One of the main criticisms of NGOs is that despite the NGO law, there is little coordination between them and often several NGOs will provide duplicate services in an area while other services are lacking.[40]

Attempts to build an economy by encouraging Palestinians to take out loans and invest in their own development have failed because of staggering unemployment, limited access to agricultural resources and stiff restrictions on the import and export of products. The socio-spatial controls imposed on the West Bank population by the Israeli occupation through the Oslo framework selectively restrict the flow of capital and hinder development in specific communities while allowing it in others. The implementation of control over capital has rearranged the relations of power within communities, reframing political issues into technical and economic and ones by providing brief relief and the appearance of social democratic participation.[41] Through a complex relationship with international donors, the World Bank and the IMF, Palestinians have in theory been brought into a globalized economic network while at the same time being physically restrained and isolated from the outside world as well as from each other. Neoliberal policies within the PA and the internationally funded aid industry have resulted in an economically dependent and indebted population. The creation of a new elite middle class through the PA and NGOs has increased the polarization among the population as well as the isolation between West Bank communities, further contributing to the social fragmentation of Palestinian society.

Figure 4 Local women in the village Assira Ash-Shamaleyya. Photo by author.

6

From agricultural resilience to food insecurity

The physical fragmentation and long-term isolation of Palestinian communities in the Nablus region have had a wide range of effects on the populations in the area. Throughout the second intifada everyday routines such as work and education were severely disrupted, as individuals were not permitted to leave their neighbourhoods and villages and, during the many imposed curfews, were also not able to leave their homes. This chapter builds on the situations resulting from isolation that have been outlined in the previous chapters and explores the various ways in which communities worked together in order to survive. Throughout the 1980s and into the period of the first intifada, Palestinian political movements formed agricultural committees aimed at helping communities to become self-sufficient in terms of food production. During the second intifada, many communities that were isolated by checkpoints and suffering from long curfews developed systems of growing their own food secretly through hidden gardens and sharing it through networks of food distribution. Many difficulties exist in terms of restrictions on the cultivation of lands in rural areas, and food is now more widely imported from outside vicinities. In looking at various examples of resilience in which individuals and communities developed innovative ways of ensuring survival, this chapter attempts to explain why, if Nablus area communities have previously been able to maintain a minimum level of relative self-sufficiency, they are no longer engaging in such activities.

The ability of Palestinians as politically and economically isolated populations in the midst of a globalized world to adapt and cope with change is paramount to the continuation of life itself. Resilience in the form of developing local ecological and social systems has made survival possible in times of the most intense isolation. Doumani has expressed how, historically in Nablus communities, 'solidarity and social networks, especially at the family and neighbourhood levels, have combined with well-organized popular committees at the grassroots level to provide the minimum necessary degree of social cohesion'.[1] In Nablus, much of the community solidarity that had been emphasized during the first intifada had largely diminished throughout the Oslo process in the 1990s and the second intifada. Declines in social cohesion have been the result of both imposed and manifested forms of physical, political and social divisions between communities, which have in part been created by Israeli military pressure which, as Doumani points out, has a 'paradoxically unifying effect on the population'.[2] Maintaining communication within communities in spite of being divided from one another was important in resolidifying social cohesion, because residents needed to work together in order to feed themselves during adverse periods.

Structural violence and reorganizing diets

Prior to 1967, the Palestinian agricultural sector was roughly equal to the Israeli agricultural sector, and Palestinians exported approximately 80 per cent of the produce grown in the West Bank.[3] Tamari notes that in 1968, half of the total Palestinian labour force worked in the agriculture sector; by 1978, this was greatly reduced as nearly one-third of the labour force worked inside Israel.[4] Despite mass labour migration of agricultural workers to Israel during the 1970s and 1980s, rural Palestinian communities, with the assistance of agricultural relief committees and volunteer student movements, brought different Palestinian communities together in maintaining agricultural production. During the 1990s, an increased dependency on the Israeli economy as well as the division of the land under Oslo and the appropriation of rural land for settlement and military use greatly inhibited agricultural efforts in rural areas. Throughout the second intifada agriculture in both rural and urban settings suffered greatly. However, in the Nablus area there have been cases of organized home gardening initiatives in some of the most adverse circumstances. Foodways in Palestinian communities are significant in understanding how the community functions, in that cultivation/production, distribution and consumption have all had to take place within the boundaries of the community, often discreetly. In Nablus neighbourhoods, hidden gardens became important to community survival during the curfews and isolation of the second intifada, and social networks were formed in order to harvest/produce food and distribute plant material in the community. Buchmann, in her study on home gardening in Cuba, stresses 'the importance of home gardens in strengthening community resilience in the politically and economically isolated country'.[5] On a community level, increased solidarity can be observed in home garden management and related community networking through the sharing of plant material and cultivation knowledge within and between the communities.[6]

Indigenous (*baladi*)[7] foods such as olives, za'tar and figs not only constitute traditional and easy-to-grow staples, but are also highly symbolic in terms of cultural and family heritage. Olive trees in particular are often passed through many generations. Vegetables, fruits and herbs that are considered *baladi* are preferable to imported seeds or foods for planting and consumption. In Palestinian villages it was common for every family to have their own specific recipes for herb and spice mixtures such as za'tar. Traditionally, foods such as wild cauliflower and thyme for za'tar would be gathered from mountaintops by villagers and brought to towns and markets, but due to the harsh restrictions on movement, imported species must be purchased at markets.

Qossay is well known in Nablus as the keeper of seeds. His tiny shop in the Old City was opened by his grandfather during the British mandate and is the only shop in Nablus specializing in seeds. He also sells his own mixtures of oils, herbs, spices and teas and makes potions and extracts for treating different ailments. The majority of his seeds are *baladi*, although he has some less popular ones that are imported from the Netherlands through Israel for more industrial farming. Most Palestinians consider *baladi* plants to have a stronger flavour more appropriate for Arabic cooking. During the invasions of the second intifada, residents of the Old City were unable to leave their homes and began growing food wherever they were able. Qossay recalled that during this time the demand for seeds was as much as ten times what it had been and that people planted easy-to-grow foods such as radishes and beans anywhere they could. As his shop was also closed, Qoosay provided seeds, often free to families who could not pay, by distributing them from his own home in the Old City, from where they were passed from one neighbour to another when a request had been communicated to him.

Qossay's shop has been the main supplier of seeds in Nablus for the last 100 years; however, he noted that, in the villages, families kept their own seed for generations. It was not until the 1990s that villagers began to come to him to buy their seeds. According to Qossay this was because after years of working in the labour markets outside of the village as opposed to sustaining themselves on their own production, many villagers had minimized their agricultural efforts and bought much of their produce in markets in the urban centres such as Nablus. Having money, villagers with family members working in Israel or in the Gulf States would travel to markets not to bring their own produce to sell but to buy imported goods. Changes in economic opportunities as well as the availability of foods in the markets caused many village families that had formerly sustained themselves through agriculture to stop keeping their own seeds, as they had previously done for generations. With the loss of access to labour markets and regular funds from the PLO in the early 1990s, many villagers experienced difficulties in resuming large-scale agricultural production. Military restrictions on land and water use and land confiscation for settlements in Area C following Oslo also contributed to difficulties in rural sustainability.

The drastic increase in violent attacks by Israeli settlers following the second intifada has had a tremendous impact on agriculture, particularly in the villages to the south and east of Nablus. In most villages that were cut off from outside markets during the second intifada, many of the agricultural lands were declared closed military zones and farmers were not allowed to access them. This was especially true in Awarta, Burin and Beit Furik, where settlements and military bases bordered the villages. In Burin, land appropriation and violent attacks all but halted agricultural production; in addition, the vast majority of the villages' farmlands are off limits to the people and most of the orchards and olive groves that once covered the mountainsides surrounding the village have been burnt by settlers. The only remaining agricultural activities are small home gardens in the immediate vicinity of people's homes. Due to siege on the village, which still continues at least in part today, and destruction of the agricultural base, the entire village remains in poverty and completely dependent on external aid.

The siege in Awarta lasted throughout the entire second intifada and beyond, until 2008. The village still suffers regular night raids and residents generally need to pass through checkpoints to enter or exit the community. Education in the village has been severely interrupted throughout this period, especially during invasions and curfews. In order to compensate to some degree, in 2002 the people of the village organized neighbourhood committees, which were formed based on a pre-existing 'mentor network', created by PFLP activists as early as the 1980s in order to educate youth in the village as well as to promote the literature of the party and Marxist ideologies. The neighbourhood committees in the second intifada, which were created to provide general education, were more organized and transparent. Children in each area of the village would meet at selected homes at various times of day depending on their age group, and volunteers in the community, some of whom were teachers, would do their best to offer lessons. During times when particularly intense curfews were placed on the village, the neighbourhood committees would attempt to find out what food products different families had more of so that they could develop a system of food collection and distribution in each area of the village, using children to carry food from one family to another. In certain areas this system worked well but towards the end of the second intifada many families became uncooperative. This is in stark contrast to the first intifada, when the PFLP had been in complete control of Awarta and food collection and distribution among other social formations were unquestioned.

Between 2004 and 2005, the prolonged siege and continued aggressive military incursions into Awarta took such a devastating toll on the population that the community ceased to function as an organic unit. Almost the entire village had been unemployed throughout the second intifada as most people were unable to leave their homes for work or school. While many families had created space for small gardens within their homes, farmers were unable to access their lands and the village was cut off from external markets. In other nearby villages in similar situations, it was often possible for residents to smuggle food and produce between communities by going over mountains at night. By 2004 smuggling food had become very difficult in Awarta due to regular military patrols in the village streets. By the end of the second intifada the community were not only experiencing new levels of poverty but, as residents recount, the character of the village itself had been changed.

Assira Ash-Shamaleyya did not experience extreme poverty at the same level as other villages surrounding Nablus, despite intense political divisions in the village and the severe siege throughout the second intifada. This was in part due to the absence of settlements directly surrounding the village. As a result of Assira's partial resilience, the residents were able to aid nearby communities. During the worst periods of siege the people of Assira would gather basic supplies such as milk and flour from the residents to store in the town mosque in order to ensure that each family had sufficient ingredients to survive. On several occasions the people of Assira had a surplus and were able to smuggle extra food in the form of aid to Askar refugee camp, which was under complete siege and invaded on a regular basis.

Throughout the second intifada all communities surrounding Nablus experienced some form of siege and restrictions on movement and access to food. Depending on the geographical and political situations of different communities, their experiences during the second intifada, as well as the outcomes, varied. Both the physical isolation of the communities and the different situations that they faced throughout the years of the second intifada have had a tremendous impact on shaping their current situations and the attitudes of the people who lived through them. Different treatment of different communities in terms of the severity of the intifada and the ability of residents to access food and other resources has contributed to the social divisions between Nablus-area communities. In Assira there is now open access to Nablus and farmers are once again able to access the majority of their land with few exceptions. In the case of Burin, the village faces regular curfews at night and attempts at agricultural activities are met with possibly deadly encounters with the nearby settlers.

Policies towards agriculture in Palestinian villages are intended not simply to impose poverty on certain communities but to control local foodways and create dependency in certain markets. For example, during the first intifada the Israeli military engaged in a programme of capturing cows in Beit Sahour; the aim of this and similar activities was not only to punish the population but to prevent local milk production, creating a dependency on Israeli milk.[8] Food production is severely limited in many Palestinian communities, and the results of the populations not being able to produce their own food or access certain markets are often that they resort to buying Israeli or Israeli settlement produce. Since the post-Oslo period, the level of food insecurity among the Palestinian population has risen dramatically despite the vast amount of international aid entering the country.[9] In the West Bank, the average household spends 49 per cent of their income on food.[10] Many aid interventions focus on food assistance; 52 per cent of Palestinians received food assistance from the World Food Program (WFP) or the UN Relief and Works Agency (UNRWA) in 2009.[11]

Nablus's urban *Bustan* and feeding the old city

Throughout the second intifada, and as recently as 2009, Nablus as a city remained closed off from much of its hinterland and the rest of the West Bank. Until 2007 the city experienced, and to some degree is still experiencing, regular military incursions, and different areas were divided often from one another. This was especially the case in the refugee camps, which were placed under their own sieges, and the Old City. The Old City was a haven for resistance fighters. Its narrow winding streets and tunnels built during the Roman period made it difficult to navigate except by locals, and as such it was both difficult to invade and equally difficult to escape. With no access to the nearby villages and very limited availability to import products, Nablus's population became dependent on food produced within the city.

A large *bustan* (garden used for cultivating fruits and vegetables) was situated in the centre of Nablus just west of the Old City. The centre of the *bustan* was flattened and easily used for the cultivation of small vegetables and beans, while either side consisted of steep slopes filled with trees, dense shrubbery and garbage. This was not by design but rather through the neglect of the owner. The result, however, was that, even though the garden existed between major roads in the centre of Nablus city, it was not possible to see into the area from the streets and from the outside it appeared more like a neglected landfill than anything resembling a garden. Despite the unspoken prohibition on alcohol in Nablus, the *bustan*, being well hidden, had the reputation among those who knew about it as a place where men would drink arak among the plants and trees. The owner of the *bustan* also maintains an irrigation system with a reservoir that is filled on a monthly basis through the city's water system and is also open to rain water.

For many years farmland within the city was common but with urban development this has slowly disappeared. Until the 1990s many of the more common vegetables sold in Nablus's markets originated from within Nablus as well as the surrounding villages. As a result of urban development as well as growing dependency on Israeli and settlement produce, this *bustan* and similar gardens in Nablus have been used less. During the second intifada and the severe siege and curfew that accompanied the invasions of Nablus beginning in 2002, the *bustan* became extremely important in feeding the population of the Old City. The Old City, more than any other community in Nablus, remained cut off and isolated from the rest of the city during the second intifada. The densely populated low-income area suffered regular airstrikes, and during the long-term invasions soldiers would occupy houses, imposing curfews on the area. In total, the Old City of Nablus spent 240 days under official curfew, the longest period lasting 151 days.[12] With no possibility of importing food and other products, and unable to open shops and markets, Nablus's population was forced to rely on one another for survival. In many cases those who owned shops would move as much of their stock as possible into their homes, and many of them would set up small supply rooms near a back window from which they would be able to sell small items to people in the neighbourhood. When someone needed something, this would generally be communicated from house to house and items could be passed through windows or, in the case of the Old City, holes made in the walls between homes. Many homes in the Old City had terraces on which the residents were able to build small home gardens using wire mesh and grapevines to conceal them. Even flowerpots became useful for growing simple and easy-to-grow foods such as beans. Items grown by different residents would be traded between neighbours, and when one family was in need of a particular item, the message would be passed throughout the city until the proper ingredients could be passed from one home to another until they reached the home where they were needed.

Ramzy was trained as a medical technician and worked with both the Palestinian Red Crescent and Nablus's fire brigade throughout the second intifada. During the curfews he would use an ambulance to smuggle food and medicine into the Old City and from one neighbourhood to another. Ramzy's family's home was situated at the border of the *bustan* on its eastern edge, also lying at the western entrance of the Old City. During the day, Ramzy and other young men from the neighbourhood would sneak into the *bustan* in order

From Agricultural Resilience to Food Insecurity 99

to harvest vegetables and herbs for cooking, often hiding between the trees for entire days until it was safe for them to return the food to nearby homes. Ramzy and his neighbouring families would cook what they had harvested together, making different dishes in each other's homes and packaging meals in whatever they could to be transported to other families in the Old City.

Throughout the second intifada Ramzy worked as a volunteer medic for the Palestinian Red Crescent. During the invasion of the Old City between 2002 and 2003 he converted a mosque into a makeshift clinic, where he worked with other volunteers providing medical aid to the almost constant flow of wounded fighters and civilians. He is one of very few surviving paramedics who worked in Nablus's Old City consistently throughout every invasion of the second intifada. Despite not having had proper medical training, Ramzy assisted in multiple emergency surgeries and births inside the Old City and at the nearby Balata refugee camp. Many storeowners would distribute leftover food from their shops, often giving food past its expiry date away for free. As Ramzy was supposed to be allowed free movement on a limited basis as a paramedic, owners of shops who were unable to reach their stores would give him the keys and allow him to distribute food to families who were in need.

Abu Khayyat lives with his wife and grown children as well as his brother's family in a large house on the eastern edge of the Old City. The house had been built by their father during the mandate period, and a variety of trees and grapevines had been planted in the garden. Abu Khayyat had studied in Bulgaria in his youth, and was an influential figure in the Palestinian Communist Party in Nablus in the 1970s. Retired and in his seventies at the time of the second intifada, he spent a majority of his time gardening. Confined in the walls of his home he grew a variety of citrus, grapes, plums and olives as well as many different herbs and vegetables. While the family was unable to leave the property, the high walls surrounding the house and thick trees and vines which obscured much of the garden from the sky made it possible for them to cultivate food in more safety than much of the community. Knowing that the majority of families in the city had no access to food, Abu Khayyat distributed grapes by passing them in packages over his wall to his neighbours and so on down the line. Throughout the curfew, whenever a family in his neighbourhood was low on vegetables or herbs, they would pass messages from one neighbour to another and Abu Khayyat would return food.[13]

Home gardens are among a community's most important resources for reducing vulnerability and ensuring food security.[14] Abu Khayyat and others with access to home gardens became very important in their neighbourhoods in providing for the community during difficult times. Smaller-scale home gardens were created on balconies and rooftops throughout the Old City, using combinations of walls, trees and meshes of vines to conceal them. Through different families coordinating with one another concerning who grew what and how much, people within the community were brought together despite the curfew, through trading food and collectively cooking in each other's homes. By smuggling food over walls and through windows and holes made in the walls between homes, and through the intimate knowledge that neighbours had of one another, the tightly knit community was able to maintain a minimum level of cooperation in order to survive.

Since 2012 the *bustan* in the centre of Nablus has continued to be a place where a few farmers cultivated vegetables and drank arak, although the land itself is a fraction of the size it once was, as a new parking area for service taxies to the villages north of Nablus has been established and new office and apartment buildings have begun construction. The fruits and vegetables produced in the *bustan* are sold in the Old City's markets, along with limited produce from villages. For a variety of reasons ranging from continued Israeli restrictions on agricultural production in Area C to international aid projects that encourage growth in non-agricultural sectors, the local demand for foodstuffs exceeds that locally produced by and available to Nablus residents. In Nablus and other centres with open markets (*hisbeh*), farmers typically bring their produce to the *hisbeh* generally around dawn. Trucks bring in settlement produce, which can be sold at cheaper prices. The result of the disparity between demand for and availability of local products is that much of the produce sold by Palestinian merchants in Nablus's markets is grown on Israeli settlements and many of products on Palestinian shelves are of Israeli origin, although they are often relabelled by the manufacturer. International agribusinesses have also decreased self-sufficiency by offering Palestinian farmers a slightly higher price for *baladi* produce than available in the local markets. This has created a situation whereby a few Palestinian businesspeople benefit from exporting *baladi* products to the global market while the majority of the population relies on low-quality imported food.[15]

Fragmenting foodways

It was through the physical isolation of communities imposed by siege and curfews that neighbourhoods and villages went to extreme measures in order to produce their own food secretly and smuggle goods from home to home. It is a result of social fragmentation and larger mentality shifts among the populations of these communities that they no longer actively seek functioning systems of self-sustainability within their own communities. The general sense of disillusionment in the villages south of Nablus and newfound apathy among urban youth are the products of a variety of changes that have occurred in the West Bank throughout and since the end of the second intifada. The long-term siege, loss of land to settlements, absence of opportunities in the community and loss of life have all contributed to the trauma experienced by rural communities, and their sustained poverty has reshaped the local character of villages which were once rich in resources. In Nablus the availability of loans and perception of business opportunities in the city, as well as an increase in real opportunities outside of Palestine for those with education, have also led to a shift in mentality, from striving to maintain social cohesion within the community to creating opportunities for themselves for those who are able.

Development projects that have focused on the Palestinian agricultural sector have largely been aimed at encouraging economic growth through the production of cash crops for export such as flowers and strawberries. At the same time Israeli border closures and taxes on exports make such agricultural business ventures more costly to the Palestinian farmers they are intended to help.[16] Furthermore, residue from phosphorous and artillery shells contaminate the soil and have adverse health implications for the consumers.[17] International agribusinesses and aid interventions in the agricultural sector have largely focused on enterprise development by determining how food is produced for the global market. This has dramatically altered the traditional peasant modes of production by forcing farmers to use industrialized methods to produce food for export. Aid interventions have caused changes in Palestinian communities by altering traditional farming practices and, with them, local knowledge and heritage, while also creating a dependency on the agro-industry.[18] Abdelnour, Tartir and Zurayk stress the need for reforms in the ways that farming is viewed in Palestine and suggest that donors should subsidize low-intensity agricultural projects in Area C directly as opposed to funding the importing of food aid.[19] On a community level, resilience and social cohesion can be formed through home gardening projects and the sharing of plant material and cultivation knowledge within and between communities.[20]

Agriculture is closely linked with Palestinian cultural identity as well as providing a majority of the income for rural communities. As lands, homes and olive groves have been passed from one generation to another, villages, agriculture and the idea of community constitute an important place in local identity. The notion of *fellah* or peasant is deeply rooted in the Palestinian narrative as an agricultural pastoral society.[21] The image of the peasant way of life has been politicized as an idealization of what Palestinian uninterrupted life should be and once was.[22] Tamari notes that one of the fundamental shifts in village life occurred during the 1970s and 1980s, when the majority of Palestinian agricultural workers took jobs as unskilled labour in Israel. In many cases this resulted in women in villages carrying on the peasant traditions in the absence of men.[23] The destruction of land and olive trees and the denial of agricultural production to rural Palestinians not only prevent communities from achieving basic levels of sustainability but are destructive to the very locus of their identity. The ethos of the Palestinian village, having its own traditional arrangements, history and forms of collective identity, is instilled in each resident to a degree that to separate oneself from it produces an overwhelming sense of anomie.[24] As communities have been divided, conceptions of identity and belonging have been severed from the larger community. Individuals reappropriate inherited memories in order to make sense of the present.[25] The constructed imagery of the Palestinian peasant and the village as the territorial manifestation of cultural identity produced a unifying effect among Palestinians in different situations. The long-term division of different Palestinian communities has caused individuals to reformulate their sense of collective identity based on their isolated circumstances. The isolation of Palestinian communities from other segments of society and disruptions in such basic processes as acquiring, sharing and preparing food has altered the ways in which different communities work for survival, and the ways that their residents articulate their own senses of collective identity.

7

Storytelling and making sense of the everyday

Communities are built on common histories, memories and heritage. The expression of collective identity, be it ethnic, religious, political or otherwise, is a vital part of the establishment of cohesion among members of any given community. Events that have occurred in the histories of communities and are then circulated through storytelling become important features of the shared memories of the community. In the Palestinian context, memories of violence and trauma within communities are regularly circulated through storytelling, and become characteristic of the community and a part of the lives of community members. The act of sharing stories within a group is in itself a process of empowerment in that it enables dialogues that encompass multiple views, allowing a community to more clearly define their place in the world through storytelling.[1] In this respect stories help people to cope with violence. 'Because violence, like storytelling, occurs in the contested space of intersubjectivity, its most devastating effects are not on individuals per se but on the fields of interrelationship that constitute their lifeworlds.'[2] Memories re-circulated through storytelling in the forms of gossip, rumours and art create local histories[3] and influence the individual's perception of their community. The trauma which exists in the social memories of communities in Palestine is shared as part of the personal histories of all of the individuals residing in it. Through the retelling and remembering of stories communities reinforce cohesion around the common experience regardless of whether it was physically experienced by the entire community, or only one or a few individuals. Traumatic experiences are 'never completely recalled or completely forgotten,'[4] which is why stories of violent events when recited at the community level not only serve the purpose of conveying information or entertaining but also become important in creating the narrative and establishing the collective identity of the community.

While Palestinians live in a variety of drastically different situations, whether in diaspora, refugee camps, urban centres or within the Israeli State, narrative and symbols create a shared imagination. Symbols of collective identity hold special significance in maintaining both a shared narrative of memory of place and political solidarity. Imagery of the Palestinian village as well as the character of the *fallah*, peasant, have become essential features of representation. Traditional ways of dress, the *kufiyya* and the dance *dabka* have all become politicized symbols of material culture.[5]

The grassroots mobilization that came to characterize the first Palestinian intifada (1987–93) incorporated all segments of the society, including women and the youth from both rural and urban backgrounds, in nationalist activities such as civil disobedience and public demonstrations as well as restructuring, modernizing and developing the modes of organization of the society itself. The mass mobilization and new social organization created a sense of solidarity among Palestinians suffering through common experiences. The popular uprising was built on the development of committees within communities, which coordinated resistance activities as well as establishing medical clinics, and providing education and development programmes in rural villages.[6] The new networks of social organization that developed through grassroots mobilization within communities transformed the society, emphasizing heavily on themes of resistance, community development and a nationalist pan-Palestinian identity. Increasingly since the second intifada (2000–6) deteriorating social conditions in many communities have caused individuals to rely on more local modes of social organization such as clan and kinship ties.

As divisions have grown in communities across the West Bank, particularly in rural villages which have fallen under the label of Area C[7] (geographically, most of the West Bank), acts of collectively remembering events in communities have become increasingly important in maintaining group solidarity among the residents living there. Stories of significant events and lost lives are retold orally as well as through performance and art, with either deliberate or inadvertent objectives of creating local legends and perpetuating the narrative of the shared experience of the community. In the following examples, it is my objective in analysing local performances within Palestinian communities to explore how various stories of events originating from within a community are later retold, contributing to the collective memory of the community and reaffirming a sense of solidarity among its members. The case studies presented here are based on ethnographic fieldwork in various communities in the northern West Bank region of Nablus. Throughout the second intifada, Nablus remained under siege and travel in and out of the city was severely restricted to the extent that people residing in various neighbourhoods and villages were unable to leave their areas.

Storytelling and community cohesion

In his essay *The Storyteller*, Walter Benjamin explains the significance of the retelling of experiences and the interaction created between the storyteller and his audience.

> Storytelling is always the art of repeating stories, and this art is lost when the stories are no longer retained. It is lost because there is no more weaving and spinning to go on while they are being listened to. The more self-forgetful the listener is, the more deeply is what he listens to impressed upon his memory. When the rhythm of work has seized him, he listens to the tales in such a way that the gift of re-telling them comes to him all by itself. This, then, is the nature of the web in which the gift of storytelling is cradled.[8]

In Nablus, the result of the siege and isolation on the different communities existing in the city, and to a much larger degree in the refugee camps and villages that surround it, has been that individuals have been forced to create logistical networks within their communities to trade basic goods and services in order to cope with the conditions imposed upon them. As members of communities with pre-existing social networks based on family relations, as well as networks formed through political organization and economic necessity, individuals share distinct features of memory and identity through their communities.

Coffee shops, workspaces and the home are all forums for storytelling and stories ranging from neighbourhood gossip, to family history, to recent loss all convey messages that reflect the atmosphere of the community. As the conditions of life in Palestinian communities have changed, so have the stories and the function of storytelling. Changes in the economic and political structures have effectively altered not only the ways in which people live, but also how they view themselves and their history. According to Hala Khamis Nassar, the most important function of the hakawati (traditional storyteller) who would wander from village to village, performing stories drawn from Arabic folktales and mythology, was 'to reinforce the collective identity of the spectators during the act of performing'.[9] In many ways traditional forms of art and entertainment have become politicized in Palestine, as have all aspects of everyday life.

Dabke in Askar refugee camp

Aken, in his study of Palestinian diaspora communities on the East Bank of the Jordan river, has noted that cultural reproduction in severe circumstances requires 'a continuous reinvention of cultural practice' and that this cultural reproduction of 'local practical knowledge … daily constitutes a community and its relationship to place'.[10] The power embedded within the sharing and expression of a common social memory was made clear to me while witnessing a *dabke* performance combined with a theatrical representation of a military incursion in Askar refugee camp that occurred during the second intifada.

Askar refugee camp is located on the outskirts of Nablus. The performance was acted out by youth living in the camp and was organized by a local community centre. *Dabke* is a type of line dance traditional in Arab cultures of the Levant, normally performed at festivals and weddings. As a symbol of culture and heritage among all Arab populations historically living in Palestine, the dance has in recent years often been adapted to symbolize nationalist unity as well as various characteristics of the Palestinian struggle. As the performance began, the dancers from the camp dressed in lavishly embroidered clothing entered the stage and performed the dance in its traditional manner. Other actors later appeared on the stage wearing plain clothes to represent residents of the camp, as well as others dressed in military uniforms and carrying guns acting as Israeli soldiers. As the new characters came on stage and acted out the invasion, the *dabke* performers either exited the stage or played dead while the actors imitated the clashes that took place. As the performance ended the actors playing Israeli soldiers exited the stage, and the dancers returned and accompanied those who were meant to be dead residents of the camp off stage. The performance ended as abruptly as the invasion had begun, as if to illustrate the open-endedness and uncertainty in every aspect of daily life under the occupation. After the show, various residents in the audiences talked amongst themselves of those who had been killed, and also of their own experiences during the invasion. The combination of the traditional dance with the retelling of this traumatic event in the community's history represents the adaptation of the traditional cultural identity to the collective identity of nationalist political mobilization and resistance, which has developed over generations as a result of the experience of a common antagonism.

The act of collectively remembering is inherent in contemporary Palestinian culture, both in the occupied territories and among the diaspora community. Events such as the *Nakba* are commemorated by holidays and symbolism throughout the fabric of the society. Significant material objects such as the keys to homes lost in 1948 kept by refugees,[11] and coins from the mandate era worn as necklaces around the throats of teenagers, serve as reminders of a shared history put on hold. In Palestinian cities streets are named in memory of the dead and the faces of those killed stare from martyr posters pasted on walls.[12] Posters and graffiti not only convey a multitude of political and social messages to the Palestinians, but they are also a record of the political events that have taken place. Through the political graffiti and martyr posters that accumulate on the walls throughout Palestinian villages and cities a new type of archaeology has been created, through which one can read through the layers of the first intifada, the second, and the present political turmoil involving the PA and tension between rival factions.[13]

Storytelling, therefore, is an important tool in maintaining identity and sharing a common history as a community. In harsh political situations in which the larger national community may be broken apart, storytelling is vital to keeping the community united against a common enemy despite internal stress and struggle. Frantz Fanon has noted the significance of storytelling as a means of political mobilization in the case of Algeria; as he has written in *The Wretched of the Earth*,

> From 1952–53 on, the storytellers, who were before that time stereotyped and tedious to listen to, completely overturned their traditional methods of storytelling the contents of their tales. Their public, which was formerly

scattered, became compact. The epic, with its typified categories, reappeared; it became an authentic form of entertainment which took on once more a cultural value. Colonialism made no mistake when from 1955 on it proceeded to arrest these storytellers systematically.[14]

The silencing of opponents of the occupation is a contributing factor to the destruction of Palestinian material culture and the denial of Palestinian legitimacy that are part of the colonial rewriting of history. Palestinian artist, writers and other varieties of storytellers have frequently been the target of censorship, arrest and assassination.

The story of Abu-Hannoud

Surrounded by a pine forest and rich agricultural lands, Assira Ash-Shamaleyya overlooks Nablus from atop Mt Ebal to the north of the city. While visiting the village I witnessed what I later learned was a retelling of a local story that was being played out by children in the street. The game that the children were playing was not an organized performance, but rather a spontaneous reenactment of a well-know local narrative. Passersby such as myself, became audience to their retelling through play. The performance took place on a roadside near a few small shops that constitute the centre of the village, with olive groves facing the opposite side of the street. The children, who seemed to be in part playing and in part performing for the crowd that had gathered, ranged in age from about eight to twelve years. They indicated scenes of battle by aiming sticks and tossing soda cans at one another as well as throwing firecrackers from behind trees to symbolize the bombs and flares used during the event that they were acting out. As the children continued imitating Israeli soldiers and local fighters in fierce clashes, the group of local men watching them talked amongst themselves of the invasion that took place, frequently mentioning the name Abu-Hannoud.[15] Much attention was directed to the boy who was playing the part of a fighter who was clearly the protagonist in the story. Throughout the game-turned-performance, which had drawn an audience of locals, the lead child hid behind shrubs seeming to be invincible and able to deflect bullets. At one point he hung his jacket on an olive tree while other boys posing as Israeli soldiers aimed their sticks at one another, and fell down playing dead. I later learned that Abu-Hannoud had been tracked by a homing-device hidden in his coat (apparently placed there by a local collaborator), and three soldiers had mistakenly shot one another as he escaped through the dense forest of pine trees that surround Assira.

What had first appeared to me to be a game of 'soldiers-and-*shabab*' (the Palestinian equivalent of cops-and-robbers often played by children in the street) was later revealed to be the story of *Mahmoud Abu*-Hannoud escaping Assira during an assassination attempt in 2000. Abu-Hannoud was a leader of Al-Qassam Brigades (the military wing of Hamas) and resided in Assira Ash-Shamaleyya. During the incident, the village was placed under curfew and more than 100 Israeli soldiers invaded Assira supported by helicopter gunships. The soldiers entered the village, setting off sound bombs and firing flares into the sky giving the illusion of night turning into day as they raided homes in search of Abu-Hannoud. The entire village was involved in the operation, either in being held captive by Israeli troops as they searched houses and positioned snipers on rooftops, or by aiding Abu-Hannoud in his escape. Some villagers set fire to dumpsters and fired guns into the air creating diversions in order to distract soldiers from Abu-Hannoud's location. Despite harsh rivalries between political factions in the community, one villager who was a Fatah affiliate hid him long enough to dress his wounded shoulder, and then slaughtered a goat on his front doorstep to divert attention from the blood.

Abu-Hannoud gained fame throughout the Nablus region after surviving multiple, as well as extraordinary, assassination attempts. As the story goes, after escaping to Nablus, *Abu*-Hannoud turned himself in to PA security forces who placed him in prison. The prison where he was held in Nablus was later bombed by Israeli warplanes after which *he* escaped again, allegedly saving the lives of three guards. *Abu*-Hannoud was eventually killed when a taxi that he was travelling in was destroyed by a missile launched from an Israeli helicopter; the footage recorded from the gunship was broadcast on both Palestinian and Israeli television networks as proof of his death to the public.

This event illustrates how communities have in some cases come together despite intense political fragmentation, and how the memory of such an event can further impact the everyday lives of individuals in the community. The children who I witnessed in 2010 re-enacting the story of what had become a local legend would not have remembered the actual event that took place in their village in 2000. The story had been retold and circulated through the community over the years, becoming a part of the common history and shared memory of individuals who were not even present during the event. Abu-Hannoud did not gain fame because he was a Hamas operative; he became a local legend because he had survived the assassination attempt and because of the local solidarity that the event galvanized. He is not remembered by locals for his political affiliation, as the invasion and attempt on his life involved all of the residents of the community equally and did not distinguish between family or political faction. This event, like others in every village and neighbourhood throughout Palestine, has been circulated within the community and retold in various circles, at times becoming exaggerated and distorted but nevertheless contributing to the collective memory of the community.

Palestinian theatre and artwork, particularly in urban areas, are widely recognized as being mechanisms of defiance to occupation and, on a broader scale, a window for the outside world to see into the everyday realities of life in Palestine. Performances and artworks produced on a small scale within communities, intended simply to retell stories from the community, can hold as much symbolic value as large-scale theatrical performances produced for the international audience in Ramallah, or the extravagant murals of graffiti painted on the separation wall. The retelling of local stories such as the attempted assassination of *Mahmoud Abu*-Hannoud holds value not only in collectively remembering the incident, and in this case an individual who became a local legend, but also in signifying an incident during which locals divided by political affiliation came together in aiding the escape of a community member despite bitter political fragmentation.

Political theatre in Awarta

Political relations within communities became especially significant in producing social cohesion during the first intifada. Awarta is unique in that it has a history of being a stronghold of the Marxist political faction, the Popular Front for the Liberation of Palestine, and throughout the 1980s and 1990s the village had a reputation in the area, as well as with the Israeli military, of being a site of strong resistance. The presence of the PFLP as a political entity in the village impacted heavily on the collective identity of individuals living in the community as well as their ability to function as a community in spite of the complete disruption of everyday life caused by military siege. As in other communities, health clinics as well as agricultural committees, women's working committees and trade unions were set up in order to compensate for the lack of civil institutions and infrastructure left in the wake of the Israeli response to the intifada.

This type of grassroots mobilization not only allowed communities to function as normally as possible, but helped modernize Palestinian communities by involving the entire community in political and logistical organization. The committees and the collective organization of the public that developed during the intifada incorporated specific political principals, as well as the nationalist ones that were widespread at the time, into the public perception of community. In the case of Awarta, these committees were mediated by the PFLP, and the political movement's specific brand of Leninist-Marxism was worked into the everyday activities as well as their stories and artistic expressions. Everything on the community ranging from political graffiti in the village to theatre encompassed some degree of political significance, emphasizing that literature, graffiti, images of martyrs as well as theatrical performances are all vehicles for storytelling, and have become important aesthetic forms of nationalism and resistance.

In 1966 the Palestinian writer Ghassan Kanafani called Palestinian literature composed under occupation a form of resistance to cultural imperialism.[16] Examples of martyrs such as Shaykh 'Iz al-Din al-Qassam, who was killed in 1935 fighting Zionist and British forces, became an inspiration later to underground organizations for armed struggle when his story was retold by Ghassan Kanafani, first in the *PLO Research Journal*, and later in the PFLP newsletter.[17] Palestinian writers and poets, most notably Kanafani and Mahmoud Darwish, have been extremely influential in terms of inspiring political movements and also the work of other Palestinian artists. Throughout the mid-1990s and into the second intifada, Toriq, an activist from Awarta, began writing and producing theatrical interpretations of stories and poems written by Kanafani and Darwish, as well as creating an adaptation of Samuel

Beckett's *Waiting for Godot,* in which the setting of the story is in the isolated Palestinian village. Toriq combined classic Palestinian and Western works of literature with the situation of life in occupied Palestine, all within the context of the small rural village. His use of the works of well-known writers modified to tell a story in a familiar setting gives aesthetic meaning to the practice of retelling stories within the community while also incorporating leftist political messages that were reflective of the popular movement which most of the community supported at the time.

> As Toriq explained: 'In Beckett's Waiting for Godot, everyone is waiting for God and he never comes, in 2001 at the beginning of the second intifada no one was sure of what was happening but everyone was waiting for something, some type of salvation. So in my version of the play I decided that Godot should arrive, but that no one would be able to agree on what he or it was. I combined the play with Ghassan Kanafani's story "The Hat and the Prophet", Kanafani's concept in this was that the hat covers a man's head from the outside while the prophet covers a man's head from the inside.'

The premise of Toriq's adaptation of Beckett and Kanafani's combined works was that an abstract object falls from the sky into a Palestinian village and instantly becomes the object of desire for the entire community. The *mukhtar* (village leader) views the object as a symbol of power and claims it as his own. The protagonist in Toriq's rendition is an intellectual in the village who believes that the object should be respected by all and owned by no one. Meanwhile a group of European researchers, played by three French activists working in Nablus at the time, feel that the object should be brought to Europe and placed in a museum. During the performance a trial takes place in which the intellectual is placed in a cage and appointed a deaf and dumb attorney by the *mukhtar* who plays the part of the judge. Optimistically at the end of the play the intellectual and the *mukhtar* find themselves in reverse positions with the *mukhtar* being imprisoned in the cage.

Toriq's theatrical adaptation of these two stories is highly significant to the situation which he witnessed unfolding in his own community, Awarta, at the beginning of the second intifada. The *mukhtar* was symbolic of the Palestinian leadership which wanted power but lacked legitimacy, the European researcher represented the international community in Palestine believing that they knew what was best for the people, and the intellectual represented the Palestinian people. The object itself, which Toriq created from a piece of painted foam, was perceived by the public as God, power or a valuable artefact, but what it was actually meant to represent was the legitimacy and determination of the Palestinian people.

Consisting of only fifteen amateur actors, twelve from Awarta and three from France, Toriq's play was performed in both Nablus and Ramallah. Through mixing contemporary events with traditional folklore and classic literature, as well as leftist political themes, the theatrical works that Toriq created reflected the collective identity of Awarta in addition to providing entertainment for its residents. Political messages conveyed through Toriq's theatrical performances represented messages of solidarity and resistance in the specific brand promoted by the party in power, in this case the PFLP, and as such invented a ritualistic representation that went beyond reinterpreting well-known stories, legitimizing the local agency of the PFLP by using political symbols. According to Bourdieu, 'ritual symbolism is not effective on its own, but only in so far as it *represents* – in the theatrical sense of the term – the delegation'.[18] In this respect, Toriq's performances acted as an expression of the PFLP's political authority in the village.

Navigating everyday life and the significance of social expressions

The significance of storytelling and memory in the contemporary Palestinian context is intertwined with the everyday experience of social fragmentation as well as the panoptic systems of surveillance that Palestinians live under. Prior to and throughout the first intifada, Israel implemented harsh policies of censorship on theatre and published material coming from the Occupied Territories, as part of a larger programme aimed at restricting the circulation of information and thus weakening methods of reinforcing cultural identity.[19] Censorship was also applied to political graffiti, which was strictly forbidden and, during the first intifada, often painted over by Israeli soldiers soon after its application.[20] Graffiti was used as a means to contest and defy Israeli surveillance, in addition to sending messages to the community such as news and political commentary.[21] Political graffiti from throughout the first and second intifadas remains faded on the walls in nearly every Palestinian village and serves as a reminder of the current struggles not only against the occupation, but also between Palestinian political factions.

Narrative can solidify a collective sense of community among a population on local and national levels. According to Glenn Bowman, all communities are '*countries of words*', meaning that conceptions of borders, territory, *us* and *them* are all articulated through forms of narrative. People imagine themselves as part of a national community rhetorically through familiar narrative and nationalist discourse. To this extent the collective nationalist consciousness that brought about Palestinian political mobilization and reinforced social cohesion at the community level was a product of Zionist antagonism. The recognition of the external antagonism towards one's society and the denial of the community form a threat to the individual's sense of collective identity.[22] The perception of the PA or other Palestinian groups as antagonist within the community creates a breakdown of the idealization of the Palestinian community as unified through an organic solidarity, which further threatens the sense of collective identity and contributes to the social fragmentation within Palestinian society, thereby weakening ideas of nationhood and national unity. Likewise, conceptions of group identity are reformulated when components of the community are perceived to no longer represent the interest of the whole. The PA, to the extent that it has been viewed as a client or indigenous extension of the Israeli occupying power, has caused divisions in communities through perpetuating distrust among the population and as such has contributed to the individualization of concepts of collective identity among certain communities. Identity can be rearticulated with social changes and when the perception of one's situation is altered. As Bowman notes, 'rhetorics of nationalist identity can only function as long as the subjects they wish to interpellate can recognise the "national enemy" as the source of violence which affect them in their everyday lives.'[23]

Making sense of place

Sharing stories of the past can recall collective memories in communities, and reignite ideas of social and national solidarity; the common experiences

Storytelling and Making Sense of the Everyday 115

of individuals, families and social groups define what the neighbourhood or village means to the people who live in it. As Jackson notes, 'the need for stories is linked to the human need to be a part of some kindred community, this need is most deeply felt when the bonds of such belonging are violently sundered'.[24] Through performing recreations of events which exist in the social memories of communities, the community addresses past events and cradle the memories of lost lives. The spectators of the recreation not only collectively remember traumatic events, but through shared recollection also reinforce the social bonds within the community. The violent act, carried out at random or with deliberation, before witnesses or circulated only by rumour, is later retold and given an audience of the community as well as social meaning; as a result, it becomes a form of spectacle. Stories are retold by different members of the community, exaggerated and at times reauthored, and given different meaning depending on the individual telling the story, on the audience or on the context of the situation in which it is being told. The same story from the history of a community can often differ depending on who is telling it for reasons of class, politics or family disputes.[25]

In the case of the circulation of the story of Abu-Hannoud for example, many residents of Assira would exaggerate the event or in some cases their role in it, although the essentials of what had happened and the essence of the story remained the same. Lisa Wedeen in her analysis of political symbols and rhetoric in Syria has noted that 'ideologues use spectacles to revise resonant symbols so as to convey current political messages. This symbolic reconstruction may entail creating "traditions" that are in fact quite new, but supposedly have a time-honoured, commonly recognized history'.[26]

As the *dabke* performance in Askar refugee camp combined elements of that which is supposed to be 'rural' and 'traditional' with that which is politically charged, numerous performative actions with alleged traditional roots as basic as the wearing of the *kafiya* as a scarf take on political significance. Because performance demands participation on the parts of both those acting out the familiar story and the audience, cohesion can be formed around the spectacle. The spectacle that is created through aesthetic displays of violence and trauma is one in which the memories of the community are communicated and rebroadcast, reinforcing the collective identity and producing a common response.

The experiences of everyday life of Palestinians involve regular encounters with acts, stories and memories of violence. Acts of political violence are exceptionally personal to the actors involved, but can also be experienced as symbolic of the common antagonism endured by the larger community. Stories of violence and trauma are retold and circulated in communities orally, and are also often depicted in works of art and performance and are thus given an audience of the community. Through performances, poetry and the retelling of stories of violence, Palestinian communities can maintain a common identity through a common experience. Through art forms and theatrical performances, various stories originating within communities are re-circulated in order to collectively remember specific events and reaffirm a sense of solidarity. Communities are bound by the common events experienced by their members, just as the larger Palestinian community is bound by the common experience of occupation. Narratives of local stories created through artistic reproductions of violence and trauma are effective in communicating all features of the community, both political and traditional. While every aspect of everyday life in Palestine is distinctly politicized, as a result of the experience of life under the occupation,[27] there is currently an increasing tendency for individuals to distance themselves from the community as a structure for maintaining social organization.

The political expressions realized in these performances not only tell a narrative of the situations of everyday life as experienced by Palestinians, but also express a specific identity related to their communities. As James Peacock notes, 'the imagination in its collective forms creates ideas of neighbourhoods and nationhoods, of moral economies and unjust rule, of higher wages and foreign labour prospects. The imagination today is a staging ground for action, and not only escape.'[28] Through collectively acting out of shared memories, regardless of whether they appear in the form of choreographed performance or children playing in the street, members of communities create spectacles of their common histories and provide an instance in which the community can share in the memory and narrative that is unique to them.

Common narratives are circulated within Palestinian communities in order to exemplify a sense of collective identity among the residents which is under threat as the communities themselves have existed severed from one another for extended periods of time. The common experience of life within one community differs drastically from that in another due to the fragmentation and isolation of once close-knit communities due to occupation. While collective identity within individual communities may be reinforced and held together through local narrative, the denial of a Palestinian nation and the segregation of various segments of Palestinian society inhibit the realization of a collective nationalist consciousness and wider mobilization of the population. The conception of community is itself an imaginary construct in that communities exist through collectively imagining the group to which individuals perceive themselves to be members.[29] Because of the long-term physical division of communities in the West Bank the populations rely on reinforcing cohesion through common memories in order to overcome the anomie that has developed from the social fragmentation throughout the second intifada.

Figure 5 Airplane to nowhere. Photo by author.
This abandoned airplane near Wadi al-Badan outside of Nablus sits as a reminder of the resident's immobility. The owner of the land purchased the striped down plane from El AL, an Israeli airline, during the 1990s with the vision of making it into a restaurant. Since the outbreak of the second intifada it has sat abandoned as the area became isolated outside of the city.

8

Negotiating space and imagery in disoriented landscapes

Following the first intifada and the Oslo Accords, a situation of two governing apparatuses serving separated but overlapping populations was formed, while creating the delicate illusion of two distinct nations and economies. In reality Israeli and Palestinian spaces and actions in the West Bank are interlinked and cannot be separated from each other. While one population exists contained, at the mercy of the other's economy and in some cases hidden behind walls, the illusion that they exist separately in two distinct spaces has become increasingly complicated since Oslo, as the notion of space itself has been contested in political decisions from Israeli settlement expansion to the annexation of the West Bank and deterioration of the PA.

The political division of Palestinian and Israeli territory has resulted in a distinction between two societies often sharing the same space; the further geographic and political fragmentation from the 1990s onward has exacerbated the separation of the two communities which exists in different realities overlapping one another. Tourism transcends obscure borders and spaces where local communities live out the realities of their everyday lives, but exist in uncertain and fluid conditions. In these spaces Palestinians often appear as politicized spectacles or are hidden either behind walls or in plain sight. As multiple populations cross through contested spaces, often with various conflicting narratives, locals who are rooted in their communities also interact with and often depend on transitory travellers, need to navigate and negotiate overlapping realities.

Overlapping realities and hidden worlds

Historically *the Holy Land* has always attracted religious pilgrims, historians and cultural enthusiasts. For centuries the cities along the coast, and particularly Jerusalem, have had encounters and interactions with a variety of peoples and as such developed a culture of trade and hosting travellers that has existed among Palestinians for generations.[1] Since the occupation of the West Bank and Gaza, and much more since the first and second intifadas, political tourism, in support of both Israeli and Palestinian causes, has become common and the territories are frequented by not only religious pilgrims but also activists, aid workers, thrill-seekers and individuals with a variety of often ambiguous purposes.

Following the Oslo accords in the 1990s, investment in the Palestinian tourism sector rose dramatically, hotel occupancy increased by 60 per cent and quickly employed roughly 1,000 Palestinians.[2] This changed during the second intifada from 2000 when the West Bank was cut off and divided by checkpoints and siege. Restrictions following the second intifada left newly built hotels and other businesses targeting tourists empty and employment among Palestinians in the tourist sector dropped by around 95 per cent.[3]

In political- or educational-centred tourism topics such as checkpoints and the realities of settler colonialism may be deliberately featured. In some marginalized and isolated villages political tourism has served not only as an income but also as protection. Olive picking tours have become popular since the end of the second intifada and served as an opportunity for foreigners to learn about Palestinian traditions as well as land confiscation. In villages near settlements foreign and Israeli activists have frequently participated in the annual olive harvests as witnesses and protection against provocations and violence from settler extremists. The presence of foreigners in Palestinian communities has played an increasingly important role in the form of international solidarity and connection with the outside world, particularly in isolated and rural areas, and in many cases reinforces grassroots resilience among residents through mutual friendships and lasting interactions.

Aqabah village of only around 300 residents is located to the northeast of Nablus in the Tubas region, resting on the edge of the Jordan Valley. The village has been scheduled for demolition years prior to annexation. Due to its location Aqabah has remained far more isolated than other villages long after the second intifada, and has maintained a self-sufficient economy, producing as much of their own food and supplies as possible. Educational and activist tourism has also accounted for 30–40 per cent of support for local development projects and maintaining community sustainability. Following the closure of international borders in 2020 due to the pandemic of the Covid-19 virus, and promises of Israeli annexation, the absence of internationals had diminished the community's already-limited economy and also raised fears of increased attacks from settlers.[4] The lack of international presence following the pandemic, including foreign journalists, did in fact coincide with settlement expansion as well as the establishment of new outposts and closed military zones in the villages surrounding Nablus as well as in much of the Jordan Valley.

On the other hand, Palestinians may also exotify themselves as historical or politicized spectacles in order to capitalize on the expectations of tourists. To this extent tourists, who may only appear momentarily and often with little background knowledge or interests in the political and social situations, and local Palestinians frequently share spaces and brief interactions, especially in places such as Bethlehem and Jerusalem, but at the same time experience different realities in those places at times involving locals creating appealing fantasies for tourists. Bowman has analysed the behaviour of Palestinian vendors in the Old City of Jerusalem and their interactions with tourists during the late 1980s and early 1990s. Young male vendors would present themselves as politically or ethnically exotic depending on the customer's preferences in attempts to sell religious or historical souvenirs, and occasionally date tourists in contests of masculine empowerment.[5]

Edward Said's concept of Orientalism refers to ways of viewing distinctions between so-called civilizations, particularly in ideas of certain cultures as being exotic or uncivilized.[6] Orientalism clarifies the dichotomy of Europe/North America (West) and the Orient (Middle East) as distinctly different, and defining ways of understanding culture and place in the world. Said explains the historical process and necessity of Orientalist perceptions and imagery in reinforcing the dominance of political and economic relations between colonial and formerly colonial powers and the rest of the world, as well as the logic of the 'non-Western other' as unsophisticated or as living fossils left behind by evolution. Images of the Arab World as intolerant, tribal and dangerous so often also portrayed in popular media create subconscious narratives that intentionally excuse misunderstandings and dismissal of Arab culture as irrational and irrelevant.[7] Said's work on Orientalism is extremely useful in providing a critical understanding of the contemporary relationships between the modern West and non-Western world. In spectacular performance and creating fantastic portrayals of historical and religious scenes, Palestinians may use Orientalist imagery to appeal to tourists as customers showing an imaginary reality, but in doing so may also exacerbate their own positions between locals and outsiders.

Nablus as a changing landscape

Nablus is a city with a long history of warm hospitality as well as harsh resistance to outsiders and violent feuds between local powers. A historical site of pilgrimage, Nablus has long been visited by travellers and researchers. Known as the capital of resistance during both of the intifadas, Nablus's history during the late twentieth and early twenty-first centuries has been riddled with assassinations, airstrikes and curfews. The suffering and isolation of Nablus throughout the second intifada had a variety of social and psychological effects on the population and in many ways reinforced the conservative and distrustful tendencies of the society. Suspicion of outsiders and internationals in the city is apparent in more extreme ways than other areas largely due to its long experience of isolation and trauma. Following the second intifada a slow increase in the presence of international volunteers or aid workers at NGOs, and later tourists, began appearing in the city. While the diversity was generally accepted as a positive and necessary development, rumours and suspicion occasionally gave way to social problems in conservative segments of the community, particularly the Old City and refugee camps. The increasing presence of foreigners also became exotified within Nablusi society, and the company of internationals, particularly women, to some degree became status symbols among a certain segment of the population. Foreigners employed by organizations and schools are also often paid more than their Palestinian counterparts, contributing to more scarcity in an area already suffering from high rates of unemployment.

During the second intifada and extending into the years of siege that followed, fighters of various political movements based themselves in the Old City taking refuge in the narrow streets hidden below congested ancient architecture, the secret passages between buildings and the Roman tunnels that remained beneath the city. In their struggle of resistance they also found

Negotiating Space and Imagery in Disoriented Landscapes   123

refuge in the people of the Old City who were in many cases the poor and marginalized members of the community. In the years that followed the siege, the easing of restrictions and the PA gradually re-establishing their presence in the city, certain aspects of the Old City's atmosphere have slowly changed.

Following economic and trade agreements in 2009, Palestinian citizens of Israel were allowed to enter Area A, including Nablus. The partial easing of restrictions brought sudden and frequent encounters with outsiders to the closed city as well as much-needed influx of money. For a time, busloads of Palestinian-Israelis[8] would fill the market streets of Nablus's Old City on Saturdays to buy spices, ingredients and merchandise for a fraction of the price available in Israel. Over the years the economic situation in the city declined and while the checkpoints remained open, except for intermittent political conflict and invasions, the presence of wealthy Palestinian-Israelis has dwindled. Housing projects that were initiated after economic agreements in 2010 came to a halt as money ran out, and still others were built to wash illicit funds, many half constructed and empty apartment buildings scatter the landscape.

Over the years since the siege and despite economic decline, the city has slowly opened to more diverse traffic, creating space for more regular interactions between different kinds of people. Both international and local investment in restoration projects in the Old City have resulted in the appearance of new cafes and guesthouses, artistically converted from ancient homes and buildings. This beatification of the Old City has welcomed a wider range of international guests while also providing comfortable places for diverse mixes of people to gather. Though the population of the Old City, however, remains the same families that have been living there for many generations, for the majority of them their economic statuses have not changed. As new cosmopolitan establishments have slowly appeared an appreciation for the heritage and history of the Old City is being preserved. At the same time the prices have increased and a process of gentrification is occurring.

Development, disparity and dis-Orientalism

Sebastia is a small village to the north of Nablus best known for its well-preserved ancient Roman ruins. The village is built on an incline with a few narrow roads winding up a steep West Bank hill. Homes and scattered olive groves line the winding unkept road leading into a small roundabout signifying the centre of the village. A café sits in the central roundabout circle where local men sit smoking narghile and playing cards, surrounding the circle are a community centre and a few small shops typical of a West Bank village. A few metres in front of the circle also sits a restored compound, the remains of a crusader cathedral, containing the tomb of John the Baptist. A narrow street twists around a few restored limestone homes and buildings of the 'old city' where a guesthouse for hosting tourists has been made. A few metres up a hill from the space, where residents live in mostly small modest homes and the circle where they may sit socializing, is a different world which seems more like stepping onto a cinema set. A brilliant white limestone platform stretches across the top of the hill to make up a parking lot where tour buses can safely manoeuvre and park. An office with the insignia of the Palestinian Authority, intended as a tourist centre, sits closed overlooking the site of antiquities while rows of magnificent Roman columns stand at the opposite end of the hill. A path leads past the columns to reveal ancient ruins of many structures including a well-preserved Roman amphitheatre at the top of which is a pinnacle from where the entire West Bank and beyond can be surveyed. Metal railings and fences enclose steep areas where people could fall. As if to complete an oriental fantasy, men dressed in traditional Bedouin garb accompanied by camels wait to entice tourists to take photos with them and to sell souvenirs. Of course the well-preserved ruins have been there for thousands of years, but safety railings, the limestone surface and the camels are all very new.

I had spent many nights in Sebastia in 2010, visiting friends and helping some local educational initiatives that I was involved with at the time. It was several years later that I would visit the village again after the area near the Roman ruins had been renovated. The parking area consisting of the magnificent limestone surface had previously been a dirt field where residents of the community would gather and share barbeque in late into the evenings while children ran and played football. The atmosphere after the restoration is clean and organized, more similar to a museum befitting of the rich cultural heritage and historical monuments that scatter the landscape; however, the people who have lived in the community for generations are now kept at a physical and social distance.

Restoration of houses and streets of the old city began in 2009 initiated by the PA local municipality to preserve antiquities and supported by European development projects. The guesthouse which was built in a converted mansion attracted occasional tourists and slowly the residents of the town became used to interactions with international guests. In 2013 the PA began projects to establish a tourist centre and construct the limestone parking area at the site for antiquities. Buses with tourists began to visit more frequently as well as buses of Israeli settlers with military escorts. From 2015 the Israeli Ministry of Tourism built safety railings along steep areas surrounding the ruins and fenced off certain areas, as well as giving brochures with information in Hebrew and English to the few local cafes trying to attract tourists. Israel's Nature and Parks Authority has labelled Sebastia as the 'Shomron National Park', effectively neglecting and denying the existence of the community living there. Tourists arrive in Sebastia by both Palestinian and Israeli transportation, but increasingly on Israeli-operated tours since investments were made in securing the antiquities sites after 2015. The Israeli military has also removed signs welcoming tourists which had been erected by the local municipality, and one of small cafes nearby the antiquities which serves both tourists and locals has been repeatedly destroyed by the army and rebuilt several times. Israeli tours to Sebastia continued during March 2020 when the PA and Israeli authorities had locked down the West Bank, and residents of the village were forced to remain inside due to the Covid-19 pandemic, while settlers openly toured the village.

In the years following the second intifada, many residents of Sebastia began to see a potential tourism economy in their village as restrictions on travel were gradually eased and occasional travellers would visit. Especially following the initial restoration projects and the establishment of the guesthouse, locals were surprised by the value that outsiders placed on the artefacts in their village but welcomed the positive attention and interactions with internationals. Jamal had always liked animals. Living in Sebastia and seeing the increase in international interests of his village in 2017 he decided to save and buy camels in order to attract tourists. After seeing the moderate success of a friend from a neighbouring village who had brought a camel to historical sites around the West Bank following the ease in travel restrictions and occasional visits by tourists who were willing to pay a few dollars or euros to be photographed with the animal, Jamal had expected his investment not only to be profitable but to lead to more international interests in his village. He spends long days in the sun waiting for tour buses; some tourists stop to take a photo riding the camel or standing next to the exotic Arab, dressed in traditional clothes, but most tourists simply ignore locals to survey the historical sites and then move back to their buses. When settlers tour the site with their military escorts, he and his animals are often cursed at and violently attacked. Jamal feels frustrated, but with five children to feed and responsible to his animals, he sees little alternative than to continue trying to attract tourists, even as Israeli authorities exert control over the area and try to push local Palestinians away from the heritage site. While international and Israeli tourists as well as settlers survey the antiquities and observe the views, Palestinians living in the community are merely presented as objects.

Sebastia has experienced dual processes of development and de-development which have occurred over the same period of time. While investment has been focused on the physical structures in the village, the population has become ever more alienated. Even with the influx of tourists in the village, the increased poverty and desperation are apparent as locals' interaction with outsiders is reduced to appearing as exotic features of the landscape. Palestinians and international tourists both play out a performance of Orientalist discourse while simultaneously existing under a complex and frequently shifting web of surveillance, politicized narratives and Israeli-dominated spatial and economic relations. Locals may act out the imagery of *an Arab in the landscape*, as performative fossils of a fanciful history, while at the same time dealing with the realities and struggles of everyday life in their own communities. I use the term dis-Orientalism[9] as a concept by which I am referring to the intersubjective state of disorientation which Palestinians experience while at the same time being presented as exotic or otherwise primitive natives. The experience of dis-Orientalism in negotiating with overlapping realities in the village landscape contributes to the overwhelming uncertainty in engaging with others and making sense of the world. Palestinians are forced to adapt to ever-changing situations and make their way through life all the while navigating the ambiguities of law, citizenship and disorientation within their own communities.

Negotiating Space and Imagery in Disoriented Landscapes 127

Palestinians use their cultural heritage as a resource in shifting and uncertain conditions for survival and to gain agency in the world. As the spaces in which they live may also be shared as public spaces, they may navigate a difficult balance in using culture as a resource and becoming spectacles within their communities to audiences with whom they share space, but become socially distanced. As individuals attempt to make sense of their daily encounters against a backdrop of shifting conditions of locating work, community, family and nation, the precariousness of situating their place in the world is a daunting task; nevertheless, Palestinians creatively respond to their changing situations just to get by in amid the haphazard trajectories of everyday life.

Disorientation of space and landscapes

The rapidly increasing class divisions in the West Bank since the second intifada and unequal investments in development and the alienation of poor and rural communities have also contributed to the social distance and isolation between Palestinians as well as between locals and outsiders. This is particularly true for young people from marginalized communities who have grown up in isolation, and likewise for Palestinians of privileged who may have difficulty in relating to those in more extreme isolation. On a personal level, relationships and engagement with the outside world may allow Palestinians to gain agency as well as opportunities in their lives. The social divisions which have developed within the Palestinian community also threaten the coherence of connections with those from outside. While solidarity and educational tourism are tools which Palestinians use to show the realities of their lives and gain advocacy, disjunctures exist in the experiences of life as it is played out between people occupying different roles within shared spaces.

The Palestinian town of Bethlehem has long been a centre of international tourism and religious pilgrimage. With the exception of the second intifada when the area was under was under siege, a regular influx of tourists rotates through the town, often staying only a few hours or days, their movement through the town is instrumental in generating the local economy. Israeli tourist companies also operate in Bethlehem busing tourists to the town for short trips in and out of the officially recognized West Bank. People living in the small town or neighbouring Beit Sahour go about their daily lives and routines, largely ignoring the crowds of tourists who are a normal part of the landscape.

The streets of Bethlehem and Manger Square in front of the Church of the Nativity are lined with Palestinian taxies while tour buses park in a nearby garage and bus station built to relieve traffic congestion and accommodate tourists. The ground floor of the bus station is filled with shops set as a market for religious pilgrims selling an assortment of merchandise with both Israeli and Palestinian symbols, much of it produced in China, to tourists who are assessed by desperate vendors. Escalators lead downwards to tour buses on the lower levels waiting to bring travellers to other Palestinian cities or into Israel. Local transportation between Palestinian cities in typical service taxies (shared vans) is also in the same location but accessed through unmarked elevators at the end of a long corridor in the back of the building, which brings locals down below the garage and further outside to a small dirt parking lot secluded from the view of main roads. The elevator doors open up into a different world where local Palestinians are literally hidden behind unmarked gates and beneath the large complex.

Israeli law and sovereignty are extended to Israelis living in settlements carved out of the West Bank and East Jerusalem where Palestinian communities exist in overlapping spaces but remain politically and socially separated through institutions and policies. In this way borders and boundaries, which are subject to arbitrary changes, function as geographic mechanisms of separation and control over Palestinian, but not Israeli, residents.[10] Likewise Palestinian localities within Israel are often isolated and bypassed by public transportation and services. Bourdieu notes that non-recognition is central to symbolic violence as it allows for the legitimation of domination and its internalization by the dominated.[11] Abu-Rabia-Queder has examined the racialization of public space through various layers of biopolitics as well as the denial language in the non-recognition of Arabic as the language of the enemy 'Other'.[12] The non-recognition of the existence and identity of Palestinians as a political community has been essential in the appropriation of territory as well as the denial of legitimacy.[13] The use of language in political discourse concerning Palestinian identity has continually been aimed at creating an imagination in which Palestinians are non-existent or at least non-legitimate. Beshara

Negotiating Space and Imagery in Disoriented Landscapes 129

Doumani has argued that the repeated non-recognition of Palestinian identity has maintained a narrative whereby the very idea of Palestine or Palestinians is delegitimized, politically as an entity or partner for negotiation and socially as the existence of the people themselves.[14] This notion of non-recognition has continually been reinforced to keep Palestinians in a marginalized position and seemingly unable to present a credible of coherent voice.

Through complicated layers of physical overlapping infrastructure, laws and regulations and non-recognition, getting through everyday life as well as locating one's own place in the world becomes all the more confusing. Palestinian and Israeli communities, policies and spaces exist in parallel realities to varying levels depending on the situations of fragmentation and containment. In daily interactions and duties Palestinians display what Scheper-Hughes has termed a 'talent for life' in navigating the challenges and uncertainties of overlaying realities and social relations.[15] Palestinians must negotiate the disorientation landscapes within their own communities and lives but in doing so create a sense of resilience which has come to characterize a distinctly Palestinian experience that is not dependent on political discourse or leadership.

9

Conclusion

Geographic, political and social divisions have been imposed on Palestinian society through Israeli controls and perpetuated through the power relations on different levels among the Palestinian leadership, the international community, different political entities and the Palestinian populations living in isolated communities. Checkpoints, land appropriations for closed military zones and settlements and restrictions on the movement of people, products and information have cut different communities in the Nablus area off from one another and have kept their populations isolated throughout and since the second intifada. Disputes and battles for power between political actors and traditionalist structures have also created political and social divisions within and between communities in Nablus. Doumani speaks of isolation in Nablus as the 'systematic asphyxiation of an entire social formation, the aim of which is to make the small routines of everyday life […] so difficult as to precipitate major demographic shifts that, in turn, would break the will to resist.'[1] The 'divide and conquer'-like situation that grew out of the Oslo Accords has, through the division of communities and political repression over certain segments of society from the internal Palestinian leadership, divided the population socially to a degree that, as in the case of Nablus, people in different communities no longer conceive of each other as the same. Major shifts in mentality have occurred in different Nablus communities throughout the period of the second intifada, particularly among youth who have grown up in their rural or urban communities with no possibility of leaving.

The experiences of life among Palestinians differ drastically depending on the area they live in, the different struggles they face and different methods of surviving that have been adopted by communities that have become isolated from the larger Palestinian society create differing sets of priorities in different communities. Depending on political affiliations, the strengths of local networks based on family and *hamula* and the presence of international organizations, different communities in Nablus have developed in their own ways through periods of isolation to accommodate their unique circumstances. As a result of dealing with different situations and isolation from the larger national society, Nablus-area residents have internalized their conceptions of national identity specific to their communities. To a large extent the collective nationalist consciousness that brought about Palestinian political mobilization and reinforced social cohesion at the community level was a product of Zionist antagonism. The recognition of the external antagonism as the source of one's suffering allows one to imagine social bonds with others suffering from the same antagonism. By defining a community based on antagonism, Palestinians were able to conceive a national identity in the absence of a state.[2] The denigration of the level of nationalist cohesion that existed prior to and during the first intifada took place through the changing political landscape of the 1990s, following the Oslo Accords and the subsequent isolation of communities during the second intifada. As a result of growing physical, political and social divisions in Palestinian society, personal conceptions of identity and group belonging have become more localized.

The surveillance and total control over life under which Palestinians in the West Bank live have profound effects on individual identity and conceptions of community. Existing in a world cut off from the outside while constantly being watched perpetuates the sense of helplessness and the paranoia that impact on identity and conceptions of community. Distrust within communities and between various segments of Palestinian society has developed through conflicting political loyalties, intervention by external actors and growing economic disparity. Widespread paranoia within communities, which rapidly increased after the end of second intifada, has contributed to the social fragmentation and breakdown of the previously existing collective solidarity among Palestinians in Nablus.

International interventions that have developed since the post-Oslo period and the rapid implementation of free trade policies by the PA since the end of the second intifada have created a paradox in which the Palestinian market is part of a global system and yet many communities remain isolated to the extent that they have minimal interaction and trade with one another. Interactions between international organizations and Palestinian communities have also altered the dynamics of power relations in communities and resulted in the creation of a new elite class of Palestinians. The class divisions that have manifested themselves since the Oslo process have created social stratification that has accelerated since the end of the second intifada. Rapidly growing income inequality, poverty in rural areas and food insecurity have been results of the unequal treatment of different Palestinian communities by the PA, the Israeli occupying power and the international community. Other developments since the end of the second intifada, such as the wide availability of microloans for employees of the PA, which is unable to pay salaries consistently, have created a debt crisis among average Palestinians in the West Bank.

The Israeli occupation of the West Bank since 1967 has had profound effects on social structure in rural and urban Palestinian society. Mass migration of the Palestinian workforce to work as unskilled labour in Israel drastically altered the dynamics of rural agricultural production and traditional peasant structures in villages and changed the relationships between rural and urban Palestinian communities. The political mobilization that took place throughout the 1980s and the first intifada again redefined the power relations within Palestinian society and organized grassroots movements in communities to work towards common goals and facilitate social cohesion in the absence of a state government. The creation of the Palestinian Authority and the Oslo framework caused drastic changes in Palestinian society. On a geographic level, the division of the West Bank into Areas A, B and C physically divided communities from each other, marginalizing those without access to Area A. On a political level, bringing the exiled leadership of the PLO into the occupied territories in order to form a pseudo-government marginalized much of the grassroots infrastructure that had developed organically in Palestinian communities. On a social level, Oslo created more internal divisions due to concentrating international aid investment in urban centres and neglecting rural areas. Development that took place in select areas was designed to foster the infrastructure of the new government. The former cadres who had been brought back from exile, entrepreneurs with international connections and former activists who had become leaders in new NGOs made up the new elite in Palestine and changed the social dynamics of the society. Throughout the second intifada the Israeli military imposed a siege on Nablus and the surrounding communities, dividing them from one another using checkpoints, trenches, walls and land appropriations for closed military zones. Many communities experienced the destruction of local infrastructure through airstrikes, house demolitions and invasions, accompanied by long curfews. The long-term isolation, as well as the unequal treatment of various communities by both the PA and the Israeli military, created a situation in which divisions between different communities developed. Political and social forces within communities have further perpetuated divisions between different segments of Palestinian society.

Political fragmentation in the context of a collective nationalist consciousness as manifested through the isolation of communities from one another has become more localized and dispersed. The grassroots mobilization that eventually led to the first intifada was driven by political parties that organized committees to see to the needs of communities and established social cohesion among the society in the absence of an indigenous government. While the period leading to the first intifada is remembered with some degree of idealization, the grassroots initiatives of the time in many ways modernized the infrastructure of small communities and also brought the population together towards a common goal of ending the occupation, although there may have been different perceptions of what the outcomes of accomplishing that goal would be. Tariq's statement that 'in Awarta we learned about George Habash before we learned about Islam' speaks of the cohesion of the PFLP in Awarta and the influence that political movements had in communities prior to the dramatic changes that took place in the 1990s. As political emphasis shifted from popular mobilization to development following the Oslo Accords, political parties lost much of their power as structures for facilitating social cohesion. As a result of the PA's inability to govern over the entire Palestinian society effectively, and the shift in the role of political parties, in many communities residents looked to pre-existing forms of social organization such as family and *hamula* to facilitate personal and local needs. With the isolation that developed during the second intifada, traditionalist forms of social organization in rural and marginalized communities gained more influence. Divisions between political movements, most notably Fatah and Hamas, further divided the population of Palestine. In Nablus often violent turf wars between fighters representing various armed groups erupted

Conclusion   135

throughout the second intifada and battles for political power and influence in the city have led to cycles of intimidation between supporters of different groups. New levels of political and class divisions have manifested as a result of Fatah's monopolization of the PA and the appointment of well-connected individuals to influential positions. Corruption in the PA and conflicts between different political groups throughout and since the second intifada have resulted in an increase in social stigma among different sectors of the Palestinian population and the further marginalization of geographically and politically isolated communities such as rural villages and refugee camps.

The social fragmentation that has developed in Nablus-area communities has been in part the result of the marginalization of political movements and of traditionalist modes of social organization being increasingly relied on in isolated communities. Exploring the concepts of divided communities and what that means for the people living in them to be isolated more theoretically, this book has looked at how living in a world of uncertainty, cut off from the larger national community, affects conceptions of self and community. Because of the long-term isolation that Nablus-area communities have faced since the beginning of the second intifada, social divisions between communities have grown and as a result cultural relationships to place have become more important within communities. Surveillance in Nablus is ingrained into the fabric of everyday life, as watchtowers line the mountainsides and drones fly over the valley looking down into the city. In the years since the second intifada an atmosphere of increasing paranoia has developed in Nablus, particularly among residents of marginalized communities, to the extent that they are increasingly suspicious of one another as potential collaborators or agents loyal to the PA or other entities. The biopolitical control imposed over the Palestinian population by the Israeli apparatus completely dictates every aspect of life, ranging from individuals' mobility to which communities are or are not able to cultivate food. Practices of control and categorization such as the use of biometric IDs and restricting segments of the population to certain areas keep Palestinians in a state of disorientation due to arbitrary and unannounced changes in the nature of the control. Paranoia within Nablus-area communities has had detrimental effects on social cohesion and the external forces of control over the lives of the Palestinian population have created a situation of profound ambiguity in everyday life. The state of uncertainty and lack of control over life have contributed to the breakdown of solidarity between communities. Due to unequal imposition of controls over different communities, social differences are exploited, creating divisions between communities and contributing to social fragmentation.

Class divisions have been perpetuated by international organizations and resulted in a growing problem of debt among the urban population. Palestinian NGOs in the form of grassroots organizations and committees organized by political parties were developed to meet the needs of communities in the absence of an indigenous state. Various forms of Palestinian NGOs were well organized and able to provide services effectively as well as mobilizing the population in political struggle. Following the Oslo Accords, billions of dollars in international aid were donated to the newly formed PA for institution building, and funding to many Palestinian NGOs was distributed through the PA. The international aid industry that has developed in Palestine, and particularly in the West Bank under the PA, invests in certain types of development in specific areas that meet donors' needs and political goals but do not necessarily serve the Palestinian population in the most effective way. Because of political interest and stipulations on foreign aid as well as the PA's own interests, only certain segments of the population are provided with services while others are not, which contribute to class differences and division between communities. Free market trade policies adopted by the PA and mediated by the World Bank and the international community have had adverse effects on Palestinian production and cultivation, as the local market is flooded with imported, often low-end, Israeli items at cheaper prices than Palestinians can afford to offer. International investment in marketing and IT sectors have benefitted urban middle-class Palestinians while neglect in areas of agriculture, production and sustainability has marginalized rural populations, thus increasing social divisions between communities. Attempts to stimulate the Palestinian economy in urban areas by making loans widely available have resulted in massive debt among many young Palestinians in Nablus, particularly those employed by the PA. As grassroots community organizations have been replaced by international aid and NGOs, and as free trade agreements have been implemented in the Palestinian economy, class differences among the West Bank population have increased, as have divisions between urban and rural Nablus-area communities.

Conclusion 137

Agricultural practices and food security are examples of how fragmentation has affected different communities in Nablus by looking at how people were able to obtain food in spite of siege, curfews and invasions. Villages and neighbourhoods that have experienced long-term isolation from one another have had to develop ways for cultivating, producing and distributing food among their residents. Because in many cases villages have been cut off from their farmland and people are unable to go to markets in other communities, villagers have had to rely on home gardens and trading with each other in order to survive. During curfews in Nablus, people have been forced to stay inside their homes for many days. From obtaining seeds for growing vegetables to preparing meals, Palestinians have had to develop systems inside their neighbourhoods for keeping each other alive. During the curfew on the Old City of Nablus, communication between different families was vital for smuggling food and medicine from one home to another. Residents used hidden gardens in their homes and networks to distribute food to neighbours. In some villages, such as Assira and Awarta, residents gathered ingredients from different families and allocated rationed amounts of food throughout the community. In other villages, such as Burin, residents could produce a minimum amount of food through home gardens but have struggled to sustain themselves sufficiently. Since the end of the second intifada some rural villages such as Burin and Awarta are now facing a crisis of food insecurity, while in other villages agricultural initiatives by international organizations have focused on exporting cash crops instead of encouraging farmers to cultivate produce for the Palestinian population. A lack of locally produced food and the flooding of Palestinian markets with imported Israeli and settlement produce have developed new social and economic problems surrounding foodways.

The common experience of life within individual Palestinian communities is exemplified in creating a sense of collective identity among the residents which is under threat, as the communities themselves have existed severed from one another for extended periods of time. The common experience of life within one community differs drastically from that in another due to the fragmentation and isolation from one another to which they are subjected. While collective identity within individual communities may be reinforced and held together through local histories, the denial of a Palestinian nation and the segregation of various segments of Palestinian society inhibit the realization of a collective nationalist consciousness and wider mobilization of the population. The conception of community is itself an imaginary construction in that communities exist through collectively imaging the group of which individuals conceive themselves to be members.[3] Because of the physical and social division of communities in the Nablus area, the populations rely on reinforcing cohesion through common memories in order to avoid internal fragmentation and to overcome the divisions and the challenges associated with the uncertainty of everyday life.

The social divisions between Nablus-area communities and the distinctly different experiences of life that people have in them have created a situation in which residents of different communities do not relate to each other. The lack of control and uncertainty around everyday life in isolated communities in Nablus produce a sense of anomie among the residents. At the same time, solidarity and social networks, often based on kinship, do continue to function on the neighbourhood level in some cases, even in the absence of the popular committees and nationalist mobilization that had previously existed. On a local level, some isolated communities have been able to maintain a minimum degree of social cohesion necessary for survival during the most adverse situations. Defining characteristics of Palestinian society and identity are very much tied to both territory, insofar as it is something perceived as stolen, and nation, as it is something denied. The common community created by Palestinians living under the Israeli occupation envisions at its centre a common antagonism and suffering of the Palestinian people inflicted by Israeli colonialism.[4] Collective articulation of suffering and the threat of further antagonism made up the foundations for the identity formation that created the sense of nationalist solidarity between Palestinian communities. Identity is not static but prone to situational reformation, as Bowman has argued: 'in the absence of perceptions of a shared threat which renders all of the members of a community "the same", those persons are likely to reorganise the discourses which constitute their identities in ways which they deem appropriate.'[5] Notions of collective Palestinian identity that are commonly invoked in literature, nationalist discourse and possibly idealistic reminiscences of the first intifada have deteriorated with the social, political and physical fragmentation of Palestinian society that followed the second intifada. As communities have been isolated on various levels and necessarily had to compensate for their situations, conceptions of collective identity have become more localized and community specific.

The geographic division of the West Bank under the Oslo Accords and military siege, and closure imposed on communities in the Nablus area, have isolated and contained communities for extended periods of time, greatly impacting on the lives of their residents. Political rivalries between armed groups and the security forces of the PA in Nablus and disputes between political parties and traditional modes of social organization in small communities have had a corrosive effect on the nationalist solidarity that had previously united the Palestinian people in political mobilization. International interventions and the free trade policies implemented on the Palestinian market have marginalized certain sectors of Palestinian society, creating social stratification and increasing division. The paranoia that developed as a result of the surveillance practices of the Israeli military and the PA has had a further deteriorating effect on social cohesion in communities and created distrust between communities, contributing to the social fragmentation of Palestinian society. The uncertainty of everyday life that exists in isolated communities in Nablus and the fragmentation of Palestinian society itself both create a sense of anomie among various populations, causing Palestinians who are cut off from one another to imagine themselves and their communities in different ways.

The experience of life within the confines of a village and the denial of the ability to leave greatly affect one's conceptions of belonging and collective identity. The forces of fragmentation that have divided communities from one another have caused disruptions in the social cohesion of communities that have been isolated, but have to some degree also resulted in communities becoming more internally dependent and tightly knit. The various layers of division and fragmentation have had profound effects in areas like Nablus in the ways in which people living in different communities have been isolated from one another, and in how they perceive their realities differently. In the context of the Palestinian village as a world, people living in isolation from the larger society are products of and agents in the spaces in which they exist. Through simple acts of shared narratives and storytelling, people create the necessary bonds and cohesion to hold onto the idea of community and a common identity. The use of culture as a resource also allows Palestinians to take control in a world of uncertainty, but also may create ambiguity of space within their own communities. Palestinians live in overlapping spaces shared with others, as they make their through everyday life they negotiate and engage in moments of interaction, in conversation as well as confrontation. Their positions within their spaces may change suddenly and dramatically, creating further disorientation in navigating their relations with others both inside and outside of their communities, as well as with the world itself.

Despite the systematic divisions imposed over a generation of Palestinians since the second intifada, and the interpersonal experience of isolation, new formations expressing a more pure solidarity have emerged. Decades of divisions which have been reinforced through space, politics and indeed class have also had a unifying effect as a new generation disillusioned by old discourses has found common ground in the rejection of the political parties which no longer seem relevant, the formal structures of the PA and indeed in any coherent leadership itself. Palestinians under threat by settlers in West Bank villages along with those in East Jerusalem have shown sophisticated grassroots resistance, and their momentum has been joined by the population of Gaza, diaspora Palestinians in the refugee camps and Arab citizens of Israel. This leaderless movement of the people has shown that regardless of the treatment of different populations and various types of isolation imposed, the divisions themselves can become a unifying factor. An emerging generation of Palestinians is unified in a common identity that transcends political and social stratification.

Humans exist as social beings, and in navigating life and coming to terms with the world around us, perhaps more than anything else have a need for sharing identity with others. While we cannot entirely determine nor can we fully understand the conditions that shape our lives, we struggle to overcome the profound anxieties that we encounter in order to take, even limited or illusionary, control of our lives.[6] Uncertainty looms over every aspect of life for Palestinians; in getting by day-to-day they invent various ways of consoling themselves through the intimacy of daily struggles and shared experience. As people make their way in the world, in spite of isolation and socially fragmented conditions and precariousness of everyday life, their relations with others become central to their understanding of place, being and futures.

Notes

Preface

1   Beshara Doumani, 'Nablus taht al-ihtilal: mashahid min al-hayat al-yawmiyya' ['Nablus under occupation: Scenes from daily life'], *Majallat al-Dirasat al-Filistiniyyah* 62 (Spring 2005), pp. 153–63, p. 161.
2   Ibid.
3   Ibid.

Chapter 1

1   Elia Zureik, 'Constructing Palestine through surveillance practices', *British Journal of Middle Eastern Studies* 28/2 (2001), pp. 205–27, p. 206.
2   Ibid., p. 218.
3   Tobias Kelly, 'Returning home? Law, violence, and displacement among West Bank Palestinians', *PoLAR: Political and Legal Anthropology Review* 27/2 (2004), pp. 95–112, pp. 97–8.
4   Bowman, '"A country of words": Conceiving the Palestinian nation from the position of exile'. In *The Making of Political Identities* (ed.) Ernesto Laclau (London: Verso, 1994), pp. 138–70.
5   Rashid Khalidi, *Palestinian Identity. The Construction of Modern National Consciousness* (New York: Columbia University Press, 1997).
6   Issam Nassar, 'Palestinian nationalism: The difficulties of narrating an ambivalent identity'. In *Across the Wall: Narratives of Israeli-Palestinian History* (eds.) Ilan Pappé, Jamil Hilal (London: I.B. Tauris, 2010), p. 220.
7   Lisa Taraki, 'Ordinary Lives: A small-town middle class at the turn of the twentieth century', *Jerusalem Quarterly* 83 (2020), pp. 79–103.
8   *Al-Karmel*, Haifa, 6 December 1914 quoted in Mahaftha, Ali, *Al-fikr al-siyasi fi Filasteen: min nihayet al-hukm al-Uthmani wa hata nihayet al-in- tidab al-biritani 1918-1948 (Political Thought in Palestine: From the End of Othoman Rule until the End of the British Mandate)* (Amman: Markez al-kutub al-urduni, 1989), pp. 23–4. In Issam Nassar, p. 228.

142   *Notes*

9   Rashid Khalidi, *Palestinian Identity. The Construction of Modern National Consciousness* (New York: Columbia University Press, 1997), pp. 28–9.

10   Beshara Doumani, *Rediscovering Palestine: Merchants and Peasants in Jabal Nablus, 1700–1900* (Berkeley, CA: University of California Press, 1995).

11   Rashid Khalidi, *Palestinian Identity. The Construction of Modern National Consciousness* (New York: Columbia University Press, 1997), p. 10; Glenn Bowman, 'The two deaths of Basem Rishmawi: Identity constructions and reconstructions in a Muslim-Christian Palestinian community', *Identities: Global Studies in Culture and Power* 8/1 (March 2001), pp. 47–81, p. 51 and 'Constitutive violence and rhetorics of identity: A comparative study of nationalist movements in the Israeli-occupied territories and former Yugoslavia', *Social Anthropology* 11/3 (December 2003), pp. 37–58, p. 38; Edward Said, *Orientalism* (New York: Vintage Books, 1978).

12   Issam Nassar, 'Palestinian nationalism: The difficulties of narrating an ambivalent identity'. In *Across the Wall: Narratives of Israeli-Palestinian History* (eds.) Ilan Pappé, Jamil Hilal (I.B. Tauris, 2010), p. 230.

13   Glenn Bowman, '"A country of words": Conceiving the Palestinian nation from the position of exile'. In *The Making of Political Identities* (ed.) Ernesto Laclau (London: Verso, 1994), pp. 138–70; Benedict Anderson, *Imagined Communities: Reflections on the Origins and Spread of Nationalism* (London: Verso, 1983).

14   Bowman, '"A country of words"'.

15   In the context of on-going occupation, Tobias Kelly has further elaborated on the dependency of Israeli identity and the Israeli state on the reproduction of a Palestinian 'other' through processes of exclusion which define who is Israeli and who is Palestinian. Tobias Kelly, 'Documented lives: Fear and the uncertainties of law during the second Palestinian intifada', *Journal of the Royal Anthropological Institute* 11/1 (2006), pp. 89–107, p. 89.

16   *Mauro van* Aken, 'Facing home: Palestinian belonging in a valley of doubt', PhD dissertation, Faculteit Sociale Wetenschappen, Universiteit *Utrecht*, 25 November 2003.

17   Bowman, '"A country of words"', 'The two deaths of Basem Rishmawi', 'Constitutive violence and rhetorics of identity'.

18   Allen Feldman, *Formations of Violence: The Narrative of the Body and Political Terror in Northern Ireland* (Chicago, IL: University of Chicago Press, 1991).

19   Salim Tamari, 'In league with Zion: Israel's search for a native pillar', *Journal of Palestine Studies* 12/4 (Summer 1983), pp. 41–56, p. 42.

Notes

20 Sarah Graham-Brown, 'The political economy of Jabal Nablus, 1920–48'. In *Studies of the Economic and Social History of Palestine in the Nineteenth and Twentieth Centuries* (ed.) Roger Owen (London: Macmillan, 1982), pp. 88–176, p. 88.

21 Avram Bornstein, *Crossing the Green Line between Palestine and Israel* (Philadelphia, PA: University of Pennsylvania Press, 2001).

22 Salim Tamari, *Mountain against the Sea: Essays on Palestinian Society and Culture* (Berkeley, CA: University of California Press, 2009).

23 Ibid., p. 34.

24 Jamil Hilal, 'Emigration, conservatism, and class formation in West Bank and Gaza Strip communities'. In *Living Palestine: Family Survival, Resistance, and Mobility under Occupation* (ed.) Lisa Taraki (Syracuse, NY: Syracuse University Press, 2006), pp. 185–230, p. 186.

25 Eyal Weizman, *Hollow Land: Israel's Architecture of Occupation* (London: Verso Press, 2007).

26 Graham-Brown, 'The political economy of Jabal Nablus', pp. 88–9.

27 Beshara Doumani, *Rediscovering Palestine: Merchants and Peasants in Jabal Nablus, 1700–1900* (Berkeley, CA: University of California Press, 1995).

28 Charles Taylor, 'Modern social imaginaries', *Public Culture* 14/1 (2002), pp. 19–124, p. 106.

29 Arjun Appadurai, *Modernity at Large: Cultural Dimensions of Globalization* (Minneapolis, MN: University of Minnesota Press, 1996), p. 35.

30 Ralph Rozema, 'Forced disappearance in an era of globalization: Biopolitics, shadow networks and imagined worlds', *American Anthropologist* 113/4 (2011), pp. 582–93.

31 Assira Ash-Shamaleyya was chosen because of its unique position and population, and because of the political and social fragmentation that developed there.

Chapter 2

1 Beshara Doumani, *Rediscovering Palestine: Merchants and Peasants in Jabal Nablus, 1700–1900* (Berkeley, CA: University of California Press, 1995), p. 56.

2 Akira Usuki, 'Jewish National Communist Movement in Iraq: A case of Anti-Zionist League in 1946' (2006), p. 212. Available at www2.econ.hit-u.ac.jp/~areastd/mediterranean/mw/pdf/18/13.pdf (accessed 15 August 2010).

3 Salim Tamari, 'From the fruits of their labour: The persistence of sharetenancy in the Palestinian agrarian economy'. In *The Rural Middle East: Peasant Lives and Modes of Production* (eds.) Kathy Glavanis, Pandeli Glavanis (London: Zed Books, 1989), pp. 70–94, p. 79.

4 Kathy Glavanis and Pandeli Glavanis (eds.), 'Introduction'. In *The Rural Middle East: Peasant Lives and Modes of Production* (London: Zed Books, 1989), pp. 1–22, p. 20.

5 Ibid.

6 Amir Ben-Porat, 'Class consciousness before class: The emergence of a Jewish working class in Palestine', *Theory and Society* 16/5 (1987), pp. 741–69; Teveth Shabtai, *Ben-Gurion and the Palestinian Arabs: From Peace to War* (Oxford: Oxford University Press, 1985), pp. 8–11.

7 Doumani, *Rediscovering Palestine*, p. 16.

8 Ibid., p. 21.

9 Rashid Khalidi, *Palestinian Identity. The Construction of Modern National Consciousness* (New York: Columbia University Press, 1997), p. 60.

10 Raphael Patai, 'Musha'a tenure and co-operation in Palestine', *American Anthropologist* 51 (1949), pp. 436–45, pp. 438–9.

11 George Bisharat, *Palestinian Lawyers and Israeli Rule: Law and Disorder in the West Bank* (Austin, TX: University of Texas Press, 1989), pp. 32–7; Tobias Kelly, 'Documented lives: Fear and the uncertainties of law during the second Palestinian intifada', *Journal of the Royal Anthropological Institute* 11/1 (2006), pp. 89–107, p. 27.

12 Doumani, *Rediscovering Palestine*, p. 28.

13 Glenn Bowman, 'The two deaths of Basem Rishmawi: Identity constructions and reconstructions in a Muslim-Christian Palestinian community', *Identities: Global Studies in Culture and Power* 8/1 (March 2001), pp. 47–81, p. 4.

14 Doumani, *Rediscovering Palestine*, p. 18.

15 Beshara Doumani, 'Nablus taht al-ihtilal: mashahid min al-hayat al-yawmiyya' ['Nablus under occupation: Scenes from daily life'], *Majallat al-Dirasat al-Filistiniyyah* 62 (Spring 2005), pp. 153–63, p. 161.

16 Doumani, *Rediscovering Palestine*, p. 22.

17 Emile Sahliyeh, *In Search of Leadership: West Bank Politics since 1967* (Washington, DC: The Brookings Institution, 1988), p. 96; Avram Bornstein, *Crossing the Green Line between Palestine and Israel* (Philadelphia, PA: University of Pennsylvania Press, 2001); Tamari 1981.

18 Salim Tamari, *Building Other People's Homes: The Palestinian Peasant's Household and Work in Israel* (Berkeley, CA: University of California Press, 1981), p. 19.

19 Joost Hilterman, *Behind the Intifada: Labour and Woman's Movements in the Occupied Territories* (Princeton, NJ: Princeton University Press, 1991), p. 11.

20 Ibid., p. 50.

21 Ted Swedenburg, 'The Palestinian peasant as national signifier', *Anthropological Quarterly* 63/1 (1990), pp. 18–30, p. 23.

22 Tamari, 'From the fruits of their labour', p. 73, Bowman, 2001.

23 Julie Peteet, 'Male gender and rituals of resistance in the Palestinian intifada: A cultural politics of violence', *American Ethnologist* 21/1 (1994), pp. 31–49, p. 43.

24 Chiara de Cesari, 'Cultural heritage beyond the "state": Palestinian heritage between nationalism and transnationalism', PhD dissertation, Stanford University, 2009, p. 39.

25 Sara Roy, *The Gaza Strip: The Political Economy of De-development*, 2nd edn (Washington, DC: Institute for Palestinian Studies, 2001), p. 94.

26 Marianne Heiberg and Geir Ovensen, *Palestinian Society in Gaza, the West Bank and Arab Jerusalem: A Survey of Living Conditions* (Oslo: FAFO Institute for Applied International Studies, 1993), p. 26.

27 Palestinian Red Crescent, 2005. Available at http://palstinercs.org/ presentation%20power-point%20curfew%20tracking%20july%202002_files/ frame.htm (accessed 15 August 2010 link no longer working).

28 Eyal Weizmann, *Hollow Land: Israel's Architecture of Occupation* (London: Verso Press, 2007), p. 185.

29 Rema Hammami and Salim Tamari, 'Anatomy of another rebellion', *Middle East Report* 217 (Winter 2000), pp. 2–15, p. 9.

30 Awarta, which falls in Area C, suffers from these conditions and it has been my personal observation that despite the easing of travel restrictions, the conditions of poverty have worsened in Awarta since I stayed there in 2007.

31 Save the Children, 'Life on the Edge', Report on research funded by the European Commission Humanitarian AID Office, June 2010. Available for download from http://www.savethechildren.org.uk/resources/online-library/life-edge-struggle-survive-and-impact-forced-displacement-high-risk-areas

32 For example, in Awarta the same electric grid and generator are being used that were in place in the 1970s, and permission has never been given for this to be expanded despite the fact that the population in the village has doubled since then.

33 United Nations Office for the Coordination of Humanitarian Affairs (OCHA), 'Movement and access in the West Bank', September 2011. Available at http:// www.ochaopt.org/documents/ocha_opt_MovementandAccess_FactSheet_ September_2011.pdf (accessed 2 February 2012).

34 Alice Rothchild, 'Pitching in for health on the West Bank', *Boston Globe*, 6 March 2004. Available at www.alicerothchild.com/alice-rothchild-03-06-2004.pdf (accessed 22 September 2011).

Chapter 3

1 Glenn Bowman, 'The two deaths of Basem Rishmawi: Identity constructions and reconstructions in a Muslim-Christian Palestinian community', *Identities: Global Studies in Culture and Power* 8/1 (March 2001), pp. 47–81, p. 51 and 'Constitutive violence and rhetorics of identity: A comparative study of nationalist movements in the Israeli-occupied territories and former Yugoslavia', *Social Anthropology* 11/3 (December 2003), pp. 37–58, p. 38.

2 Joost Hiltermann, *Behind the Intifada: Labour and Woman's Movements in the Occupied Territories* (Princeton, NJ: Princeton University Press, 1991), pp. 53, 57.

3 This is important in understanding how antagonism was responded to differently in different areas, as well as how rural areas took it upon themselves to develop social networks based on the needs of the community. In Awarta for example, the woman's working committee was run by the PFLP during the intifada; it exists in name only as there is currently no community centre in Awarta where women are able to gather. In discussing the role of women in Awarta with current and former residents, it seems as if it has grown significantly more conservative than what has been described to me in terms of activities throughout the 1980s and 1990s.

4 Rema Hammami and Salim Tamari, 'Populist paradigms: Palestinian sociology', *Contemporary Sociology: A Journal of Reviews* 26/3 (May 1997), pp. 275–9, p. 277.

5 Iris Jean-Klein, 'Nationalism and resistance: The two faces of everyday activism during the intifada', *Cultural Anthropology* 16/1 (2001), pp. 83–166, p. 83.

6 Susan Slyomovics, '"To put one's fingers in the bleeding wound": Palestinian theatre under Israeli censorship', *TDR (1988–)* 35/2 (1991), pp 18–38, p. 18.

7 Glenn Bowman, '"A country of words": Conceiving the Palestinian nation from the position of exile'. In *The Making of Political Identities* (ed.) Ernesto Laclau (London: Verso, 1994), pp. 138–70.

8 2012 Interview with Bashar in Beit Furik.

9 Iris Jean-Klein, 'Into committees, out of the house? Familiar forms in the organization of Palestinian committee activism during the first intifada', *American Ethnologist* 30/4 (2003), pp. 556–77, p. 556.

Notes

10 Hiltermann, *Behind the Intifada*, pp. 53, 57.

11 Naseef Muallem, 'The future of the left in Palestine', Paper prepared for the Palestinian Centre for Peace and Democracy (PCPD) (2009), p. 5. Available for download at www.rosalux.de/fileadmin/rls_uploads/.../Beitrag_Naseef_Muallem.pdf (accessed 15 August 2012).

12 2012 interview with Sameer in Awarta.

13 2012 interview with Abu Ahmad in Aqraba.

14 Graham Usher, 'The politics of internal security: The PA's new intelligence services', *Journal of Palestine Studies* 25/2 (1996), pp. 21–34, p. 32.

15 Ibid., p. 25.

16 Crisis Group Report 2009. In-depth discussion of politically affiliated gangs elsewhere in the Arab world can be found in Philip Khoury and Joseph Kostiner (eds), *Tribes and State Formation in the Middle East* (Berkeley, CA: University of California Press, 1990).

17 Jamil Hilal, 'The polarization of the Palestinian political field', *Journal of Palestine Studies* 39/3 (2010), pp. 24–39.

18 Ibid., p. 28.

19 Jamil Hilal, 'Hamas's rise as charted in the polls, 1994–2005', *Journal of Palestine Studies* 35/3 (2006), pp. 6–19.

20 Rema Hammami and Salim Tamari, 'Anatomy of another rebellion', *Middle East Report* 217 (Winter 2000), pp. 2–15, pp. 2–3.

21 Frantz Fanon, 'National culture', from 'On national culture' and 'The pitfalls of national consciousness' [1961]. In *The Wretched of the Earth*, trans. Constance Farrington (New York: Grove Press, 1968), p. 156.

22 Usher, 'The politics of internal security', p. 32.

23 Hilal, 'The polarization of the Palestinian political field', p. 31.

24 While the PA is limited in the services that it is able to provide in Area C, into which most villages fall, there still exists an atmosphere of surveillance. This is due to the large-scale employment of family members of those loyal to the PA as well as other attempts that are made towards population control.

25 2012 interview with Sameer in Awarta.

26 Slyomovics, '"To put one's fingers in the bleeding wound"', p. 32.

27 Julie Peteet, 'The writing on the walls: The graffiti of the Intifada', *Cultural Anthropology* 11/2 (1996), pp. 139–59.

28 Ibid., pp. 140–3.

29 Usher, 'The politics of internal security'.

30 Hilal, 'The polarization of the Palestinian political field', pp. 24–39.

31 Ibid., p. 36.

32 Ibid., p. 35

33 Taraki, *Palestinian Society*, p. 1.

34 Lisa Wedeen, *Ambiguities of Domination: Politics, Rhetoric, and Symbols in Contemporary Syria* (Chicago, IL: University of Chicago Press, 1999), p. 14.

35 Salim Tamari, 'Left in limbo: Leninist heritage and Islamist challenge', *Middle East Report* 179 (November–December 1992), pp. 16–21.

36 Ibid., p. 21.

37 Muallem, 'The future of the left in Palestine', pp. 5, 7.

38 Salim Tamari, *Mountain against the Sea: Essays on Palestinian Society and Culture* (Berkeley, CA: University of California Press, 2009).

39 Lisa Taraki, 'Ordinary Lives: A small-town middle class at the turn of the twentieth century', *Jerusalem Quarterly* 83 (2020), pp. 79–103.

40 Hilal, 'The polarization of the Palestinian political field', p. 32.

41 Glenn Robinson, 'The role of the professional middle class in the mobilization of Palestinian society: The medical and agricultural committees', *International Journal of Middle East Studies* 25/2 (May 1993), pp. 301–26, pp. 301–13.

42 Ibid.

43 Rex Brynen, 'The dynamics of Palestinian elite formation', *Journal of Palestine Studies* 24/3 (1995), pp. 31–43, p. 33.

44 Robinson, 'The role of the professional middle class', p. 301.

45 Fanon 'National culture', p. 156.

46 Sarab Abu-Rabia-Queder, 'The biopolitics of declassing Palestinian professional women in a settler-colonial context', *Current Sociology* 67/1 (2019), p 146.

47 Issam Nassar, 'Palestinian nationalism: The difficulties of narrating an ambivalent identity'. In *Across the Wall: Narratives of Israeli-Palestinian History* (eds.) Ilan Pappé, Jamil Hilal (London: I.B. Tauris, 2010), p. 230.

48 Ibid.

49 Jean-Klein, 'Nationalism and resistance', p. 84.

50 Tobias Kelly, 'The Palestinian legal system and the fragmentation of coercive power', Crisis States Programme working papers series 1, 41, Crisis States Research Centre, London School of Economics and Political Science (2004), p. 16.

51 Rashid Khalidi, *The Hundred Years' War on Palestine: A History of Settler Colonialism and Resistance, 1917–2017* (London: Profile Books Ltd, 2020).

Chapter 4

1 Beshara Doumani, 'Nablus taht al-ihtilal: mashahid min al-hayat al-yawmiyya' ['Nablus under occupation: Scenes from daily life'], *Majallat al-Dirasat al-Filistiniyyah* 62 (Spring 2005), pp. 153–63, p. 153.

2 Akira Usuki, 'Jewish National Communist Movement in Iraq: A case of anti-Zionist League in 1946' (2006), p. 212. Available at www2.econ.hit-u. ac.jp/~areastd/mediterranean/mw/pdf/18/13.pdf (accessed 8 March 2015), p. 212; see also Glenn Bowman, 'The two deaths of Basem Rishmawi: Identity constructions and reconstructions in a Muslim-Christian Palestinian community', *Identities: Global Studies in Culture and Power* 8/1 (March 2001), pp. 47–81 and 'Constitutive violence and rhetorics of identity: A comparative study of nationalist movements in the Israeli-occupied territories and former Yugoslavia', *Social Anthropology* 11/3 (December 2003), pp. 37–58.

3 Joost Hiltermann, *Behind the Intifada: Labour and Woman's Movements in the Occupied Territories* (Princeton, NJ: Princeton University Press, 1991), pp. 53–7; Salim Tamari, 'Left in limbo: Leninist heritage and Islamist challenge', *Middle East Report* (November–December 1992), pp. 16–21, p. 19.

4 Lisa Taraki, *Palestinian Society: Contemporary Realities and Trends: Palestinian Women: A Status Report*, vol. 1 (Birzeit: Women's Studies Program, Birzeit University, 1998), p. 7.

5 Ibid.

6 Ibid., p. 2.

7 Marianne Heiberg and Geir Ovensen, *Palestinian Society in Gaza, the West Bank and Arab Jerusalem: A Survey of Living Conditions* (Oslo: FAFO Institute for Applied International Studies, 1993), p. 244.

8 Penny Johnson, 'Living together in a nation of fragments: Dynamics of kin, place, and nation'. In *Living Palestine: Family Survival, Resistance, and Mobility Under Occupation* (ed.) Lisa in Taraki (Syracuse, NY: Syracuse University Press, 2006), p. 60.

9 Ibid., p. 99.

10 Ibid., p. 61.

11 Rema Hammami, 'Women in Palestinian society'. In *Palestinian Society in Gaza, the West Bank and Arab Jerusalem: A Survey of Living Conditions* (eds.) Marianne Heiberg, Geir Ovensen (Oslo: FAFO Institute for Applied International Studies, 1993), pp. 283–311, p. 286.

12 There is a very prevalent and widely expressed feeling of both neglect and rejection from the PA and the larger Palestinian community in Awarta which has been explained by some residents to me as being punishment for the village's deep relationship with the PFLP and their relative self-sufficiency until halfway through the second intifada.

13 Michel Foucault, *The Will to Knowledge: The History of Sexuality Volume One*, trans. Robert Hurley (London: Penguin, 1998), pp. 137–8.

14 Sarab Abu-Rabia-Queder, 'The biopolitics of declassing Palestinian professional women in a settler-colonial context', *Current Sociology* 67/1 (2019), pp. 141–58.

15 Helga Tawil-Souri, 'Colored identity: The politics and materiality of ID cards in Palestine/Israel', *SocialText* 29/2 (2011), pp. 67–97, p. 90.

16 Michel Foucault, *Discipline and Punish: The Birth of the Prison* (London: Penguin, 1975), p. 90.

17 Nir Gazit, 'Social agency, spatial practices, and power: The micro-foundations of fragmented sovereignty in the Occupied Territories', *International Journal of Politics, Culture and Society* 22 (2009), pp. 83–103, pp. 85–7.

18 Ibid., p. 88.

19 Talal Asad, 'On torture, or cruel, inhuman, and degrading treatment'. In *Social Suffering* (eds.) Arthur Kleinman, Veena Das, Margaret M. Lock (Berkeley, CA: University of California Press, 1997), pp. 285–307, p. 288.

20 Foucault, *Discipline and Punish*, p. 205.

21 Gilles Deleuze, 'Postscript on the societies of control', *October* 59 (Winter 1992), pp. 3–7, p. 6.

22 Nashif Nadim and Marwa Fatafta, 'Surveillance of Palestinians and the fight for digital rights'. *Al-Shabaka Policy Brief* (2017).

23 Ibid., pp. 2–3.

24 Johnson, 'Living together in a nation of fragments', p. 99.

25 Ibid.

26 Bourdieu, *Algeria 1960*, p. 50.

27 Michael Taussig, *The Nervous System* (New York: Routledge, 1992), p. 17.

28 Ibid., p. 13.

29 Bourdieu, *Algeria 1960*, p. 61.

30 Glenn Bowman, '"A country of words": Conceiving the Palestinian nation from the position of exile'. In *The Making of Political Identities* (ed.) Ernesto Laclau (London: Verso, 1994), pp. 138–70.

Chapter 5

1 Joost Hilterman, *Behind the Intifada: Labour and Woman's Movements in the Occupied Territories* (Princeton, NJ: Princeton University Press, 1991), p. 11.

2 Salim Tamari, 'Left in limbo: Leninist heritage and Islamist challenge', *Middle East Report* (November–December 1992), pp. 16–21, p. 19.

3 Helga Tawil-Souri, 'Marginalizing Palestinian development: Lessons against peace', *Development* 49/2 (2006), pp. 75–80, p. 76.

4 Rex Brynen, 'A critical assessment of international aid to the West Bank and Gaza', *Journal of Palestine Studies* 25/3 (1996), pp. 79–92 and *A Very Political Economy: Peacebuilding and Foreign Aid in the West Bank and Gaza* (Washington, DC: United States Institute of Peace Studies, 1996); Chiara de Cesari, 'Cultural heritage beyond the "state": Palestinian heritage between nationalism and transnationalism', PhD dissertation, Stanford University, 2009; Jamil Hilal, 'The effect of the Oslo Agreement on the Palestinian political system'. In *After Oslo: New Realities, Old Problems* (eds.) George Giacaman, Dag Jorund Lonning (London: Pluto Press, 1998), pp. 121–45; Glenn Robinson, *Building a Palestinian State* (Bloomington, IN: Indiana University Press 1997); Sara Roy, *The Gaza Strip: The Political Economy of De-development*, 2nd edn (Washington, DC: Institute for Palestinian Studies, 2001).

5 De Cesari, 'Cultural heritage beyond the "state"', p. 56.

6 Ibid., p. 57; Brynen, 'A critical assessment of international aid'.

7 Brynen, *A Very Political Economy*, p. 19.

8 Hilterman, *Behind the Intifada*, p. 12.

9 Sari Hanafi and Linda Tabari, 'The new Palestinian globalized elite', *Jerusalem Quarterly* 24 (2005), pp. 13–32, p. 21.

10 Islah Jad, 'NGOs: Between buzzwords and social movements', *Development in Practice* 17/4–5 (August 2007), pp. 622–9, pp. 622–4.

11 Rema Hammami, 'Palestinian NGOs since Oslo: From NGO politics to social movements?', *Middle East Report* 214 (Spring 2000), pp. 16–19, 27, 48.

12 De Cesari, 'Cultural heritage beyond the "state"', 2009.

13 Denis Joseph Sullivan, 'NGOs in Palestine: Agents of development and foundation of civil society', *Journal of Palestine Studies* 25/3 (1996), pp. 93–100.

14 Jad, 'NGOs'.

15 Nathan J. Brown, *Palestinian Politics after the Oslo Accords: Resuming Arab Palestine* (Berkeley, CA: University of California Press, 2003), p. 138.

16 Hammami, 'Palestinian NGOs since Oslo'; Robinson, *Building a Palestinian State*; Rex Brynen, 'The dynamics of Palestinian elite formation', *Journal of Palestine Studies* 24/3 (1995), pp. 31–43.

17 Hammami, 'Palestinian NGOs since Oslo', p. 16.

18 Robinson, *Building a Palestinian State*.

19 Hammami, 'Palestinian NGOs since Oslo', p. 27.

20 Ibid.

21 Tawil-Souri, 'Marginalizing Palestinian development', p. 78.

22 Ibid., p. 77.

23 Jeremy Wildeman, 'NGO hush money: Trading silence for access and privilege', *thinkIR*, 30 January 2012. Available at http://www.thinkir.co.uk/ngo-hush-money/ (accessed 15 March 2012).

24 Aisha Mansour, 'Impact of Post Oslo aid interventions on the Palestinian agricultural sector', Masters dissertation, Bethlehem University, 2012.

25 Alaa Tartir, Sam Bahour and Samer Abdelnour, 'Defeating dependency, creating a resistance economy', policy brief, Al-Shabaka, Washington, DC (2012), p. 3.

26 Ibid., p. 5.

27 United States Agency for International Development (USAID), 'The NGO mapping project: A new approach to advancing Palestinian civil society', Report for the Center for the Study of the Presidency, 2008, pp. 8–9. Available at http://pdf.usaid.gov/pdf_docs/PNADO474.pdf (accessed 15 October 2012).

28 Ibid.

29 Philip Leech, 'Why Jabal An-Nar? Researching Nablus', *Bulletin for the Council for British Research in the Levant* 7, no. 1 (2012): 30–5.

30 Raja Khalidi and Sobhi Samour, 'Neoliberalism as liberation: The statehood program and the remaking of the Palestinian national movement', *Journal of Palestine Studies* 40/2 (2011), pp. 6–25, p. 20.

31 Hanafi and Tabari, 'The new Palestinian globalized elite'.

32 David Harvey, *Spaces of Capital: Towards a Critical Geography* (Edinburgh: Edinburgh University Press, 2001), p. 332.

33 Khalidi and Samour, 'Neoliberalism as liberation', p. 7.

34 Samer Abdelnour, Alaa Tartir and Rami Zurayk, 'Farming Palestine for freedom', Policy brief, Al-Shabaka, Washington DC, July 2012.

35 America-Mideast Educational and Training Services Inc.

36 Pierre Bourdieu, *Algeria 1960: The Disenchantment of the World, the Sense of Honour, the Kabyle House or the World Reversed* (Cambridge: Cambridge University Press, 1972), p. 13.

Notes

37 Ibid., p. 3.

38 Frank Barat, 'We've gone way beyond apartheid', Interview with Jeff Hapler, *The New Internationalist*, 26 April 2012.

39 Jad, 'NGOs', p. 624.

40 USAID, 'The NGO mapping project'.

41 Sara Roy, 'The Palestinian-Israeli conflict and Palestinian socioeconomic decline: A place denied', *International Journal of Politics, Culture, and Society* 17/3 (Spring 2004), pp. 365–6.

Chapter 6

1 Beshara Doumani, 'Nablus taht al-ihtilal: mashahid min al-hayat al-yawmiyya' ['Nablus under occupation: Scenes from daily life'], *Majallat al-Dirasat al-Filistiniyyah* 62 (Spring 2005), pp. 153–63, p. 153.

2 Ibid.

3 Applied Research Institute of Jerusalem (ARIJ), *A Review of the Palestinian Agricultural Sector* (2007). Available from www.arij.org/files/admin/2007_agricutlure_sector_review_arabic_lr.pdf

4 Salim Tamari, *Building Other People's Homes: The Palestinian Peasant's Household and Work in Israel* (Berkeley, CA: University of California Press, 1981), pp. 33–7.

5 Christine Buchmann, 'Cuban home gardens and their role in social-ecological resilience', *Human Ecology* 37 (August 2009), pp. 705–21, p. 705.

6 Ibid., p. 718.

7 *Baladi* ([of] my country) is used to describe plants indigenous to Palestine.

8 Samer Abdelnour, Alaa Tartir and Rami Zurayk, 'Farming Palestine for freedom', Policy brief, Al-Shabaka, Washington DC, July 2012, p. 3.

9 Aisha Mansour, 'Impact of Post Oslo aid interventions on the Palestinian agricultural sector', Masters dissertation, Bethlehem University, 2012.

10 World Food Program (WFP) and Food and Agriculture Organization (FAO), *Socio-economic and Food Security Survey Report, West Bank* (Jerusalem: WFP/FAO, 2009), p. 6.

11 Palestinian Economic Policy and Research Institute (MAS), 'Quarterly economic and social monitor' (November 2010) vol. 22, p. 5.

12 United Nations Office for the Coordination of Humanitarian Affairs (OCHA), 'Movement and access in the West Bank', September 2011. Available at http://

www.ochaopt.org/documents/ocha_opt_MovementandAccess_FactSheet_September_2011.pdf (accessed 15 October 2012).

13   It is worth noting that while many individuals in Nablus who maintained home gardens during the intifada have since stopped, Abu Khayyat continues to maintain his garden, and his household of eleven rarely has the need to purchase vegetables, herbs and fruits.

14   Buchmann, 'Cuban home gardens'.

15   Mansour, 'Impact of Post Oslo aid interventions', p. 38.

16   Alaa Tartir, Sam Bahour and Samer Abdelnour, 'Defeating dependency, creating a resistance economy', Policy brief, Al-Shabaka, Washington, DC (2012), p. 6.

17   Ibid., p. 2.

18   Michael Kearney, *Reconceptualizing the Peasantry. Anthropology in Global Perspective* (Boulder, CO: Westview Press, 1996), pp. 127–9.

19   Abdelnour, Tartir and Zurayk, 'Farming Palestine for freedom', p. 8.

20   Buchmann, 'Cuban home gardens', p. 718.

21   *Mauro Van* Aken, 'Facing home: Palestinian belonging in a valley of doubt', PhD dissertation, Faculteit Sociale Wetenschappen, Universiteit *Utrecht*, 25 November 2003, p. 88.

22   Ted Swedenburg, 'The Palestinian peasant as national signifier', *Anthropological Quarterly* 63/1 (1990), pp. 18–30.

23   Tamari, *Building Other People's Homes*.

24   Glenn Bowman, 'Constitutive violence and rhetorics of identity: A comparative study of nationalist movements in the Israeli-occupied territories and former Yugoslavia', *Social Anthropology* 11/3 (December 2003), pp. 37–58, p. 39.

25   Loren Lybarger, *Identity and Religion in Palestine: The Struggle between Islamism and Secularism in the Occupied Territories* (Princeton, NJ: Princeton University Press, 2007), p. 16.

Chapter 7

1   Michael Jackson, *The Politics of Storytelling: Violence, Transgression and Intersubjectivity* (Copenhagen: Museum Tusclanum Press, 2002), p. 39.

2   Ibid.

Notes

3   Veena Das, *Life and Worlds: Violence and the Descent into the Ordinary* (Berkeley: University of California Press, 2007), p. 109.

4   Antonius Robben, *How Traumatized Societies Remember: The Aftermath of Argentina's Dirty War* (Cultural Critique, 2005 no. 59), p. 122.

5   Issam Nassar, 'Palestinian nationalism: The difficulties of narrating an ambivalent identity'. In *Across the Wall: Narratives of Israeli-Palestinian History* (eds.) Ilan Pappé, Jamil Hilal (London: I.B. Tauris, 2010), p. 227.

6   Salim Tamari, 'Left in limbo: Leninist heritage and Islamist challenge', *Middle East Report* 179 (November–December 1992), p. 19. Joost Hiltermann, *Behind the Intifada: Labour and Woman's Movements in the Occupied Territories* (Princeton, NJ: Princeton University Press 1991), pp. 53–7.

7   Following the signing of the Oslo Accords in 1993 and the creation of the PA, the West Bank was divided into three distinct areas. 'Area A' is the built up urban areas constituting only 17 per cent of the West Bank and is where the PA is in charge of security and civil administration. The PA and Israeli military jointly control 'Area B' which is 24 per cent of the land, consisting of mostly villages. 'Area C', 59 per cent of the West Bank, is under the complete control of the Israeli military. Most rural areas fall under the category of 'Area C'.

8   Walter Benjamin, trans. Zohn, Harry, 'The story-teller: Reflections on the works of Nicolai Leskov', *Chicago Review* 16/1 (Winter–Spring, 1963), p. 87.

9   Hala Khamis Nassar, 'Stories from under occupation: Performing the Palestinian experience', *Theatre Journal* 58/1 (2006), p. 22.

10   *Mauro Van* Aken, 'Facing home: Palestinian belonging in a valley of doubt', PhD dissertation, Faculteit Sociale Wetenschappen, Universiteit *Utrecht 2003.*

11   Lori Allen, 'Getting by the occupation: How violence became normal during the Second Intifada', *Cultural Anthropology* 23 (2008), p. 461.

12   Ibid., p. 456.

13   Ibid., p. 468.

       Julie Peteet, 'The writing on the walls: The graffiti of the intifada', *Cultural Anthropology* 11/2 (1996), p. 139.

14   Frantz Fanon, *'National Culture.' From 'On National Culture' and 'The Pitfalls of National Consciousness' [1961] in The Wretched of the Earth*, trans. Constance Farrington (New York: Grove Press, 1968), p. 155.

15   After witnessing this performance and realizing that it held local significance deeper than that of a child's game, I conducted interviews with locals and

searched for archived news articles regarding the attempted assassination of Mahmoud Abu-Hannoud.

16 Susan Slyomovics, 'To put one's fingers in the bleeding wound': Palestinian theatre under Israeli censorship', *TDR* 35/2 (1988–1991), p. 18. Barbara Harlow, *Resistance Literature* (New York: Methuen, 1987).

17 Rashid Khalidi, *Palestinian Identity. The Construction of Modern National Consciousness* (New York: Columbia University Press, 1997), p. 195.

18 Pierre Bourdieu, *Language and Symbolic Power*, ed. JB Thompson, trans. G. Raymond and M. Adamson (Cambridge, MA: Harvard University 1991), p. 115.

19 Slyomovics, 'To Put One's Fingers in the Bleeding Wound', p. 32

20 Julie Peteet, 'The writing on the walls: The graffiti of the intifada', *Cultural Anthropology* 11/2 (1996), pp. 139–59.

21 Ibid., pp. 140–3.

22 Glenn Bowman, '"A country of words": Conceiving the Palestinian nation from the position of exile'. In *The Making* of *Political Identities* (ed.) E. Laclau (London: Verso, 1994), pp. 138–170.

   Glenn Bowman, *The Two Deaths of Basem Rishmawi: Identity Constructions and Reconstructions in a Muslim-Christian Palestinian Community* (From Identities: Global Studies in Culture and Power, March 2001), VIII:1, pp. 47–81.

23 Glenn Bowman, 'Constitutive violence and rhetorics of identity: A comparative study of nationalist movements in the Israeli-occupied territories and former Yugoslavia', *Journal of the European Association of Social Anthropologist* XI (3 December 2003), p. 46.

24 Michael Jackson, *The Politics of Storytelling: Violence, Transgression and Intersubjectivity* (Copenhagen: Museum Tusclanum Press, 2002), p. 33.

25 Michael Gilsenan, *Lords of the Lebanese Marches: Violence and Narrative in an Arab Society* (London: I.B. Tauris Publishers, 1996), pp. 57–111.

26 Lisa Wedeen, *Ambiguities of Domination: Politics, Rhetoric, and Symbols in Contemporary Syria* (Chicago: University of Chicago Press, 1999), p. 13.

27 Iris Jean-Klein, 'Nationalism and resistance: The two faces of everyday activism during the intifada', 16/1 *Cultural Anthropology* (2001), p. 84.

28 James L. Peacock, *Rites of Modernization: Symbolic and Social Aspects of Indonesian Proletarian Drama* (Chicago: University of Chicago Press, 1968).

29 Bowman, '"A country of words"', pp. 266.

   Benedict Anderson, *Imagined Communities: Reflections On the Origins and Spread of Nationalism* (London: Verso 1983).

Chapter 8

1   Salim Tamari, *Mountain against The Sea: Essays on Palestinian Society and Culture* (Berkeley: University of California Press, 2008).

2   Rami Kassis, 'The struggle for justice through tourism in Palestine'. In *Peace through Tourism* (London: Routledge, 2013), pp. 245–60.

3   Ibid.

    Jennifer Lynn Kelly, 'Asymmetrical itineraries: Militarism, tourism, and solidarity in occupied Palestine', *American Quarterly* 68/3 (2016), pp. 723–45.

4   June 2020 interview with Aqabah Mayor Haj Sami Sadeq.

5   Glenn Bowman, *Passion, Power & Politics in a Palestinian Tourist Market.* In *The Tourist Image: Myths and Myth Making in Tourism* (ed.) Selwyn, Tom (Chichester: Wiley, 1996), pp. 83–104.

6   Edward Said, *Orientalism* (New York: Vintage Books, 1978).

7   Ibid., p. 108

8   I use the term 'Palestinian-Israeli' to refer to Palestinian citizens of Israel more commonly referred to as 'Israeli Arabs' or among many Palestinian circles as 'Palestinians from 1948.'

9   Gannit Ankori uses the term dis-Orientalism in examining Palestinian art over different periods to refer to 'the self-empowerment of oriental artists' while also referring to the sense of loss and displacement of the Palestinian people following the Nakba. Olga González has expanded on this term in discussing representations of occupation, oppression and reterritorialization as features of Palestinian art as representations of political and collective displacement. I use the term here more as a concept by which I am referring to the intersubjective state of disorientation which Palestinians experience while at the same time being presented as exotic or otherwise primitive natives.

    Gannit Ankori, Palestinian art. Reaktion books, 2013, pp. 17–20.

    Olga González, 'Culture and politics in the visual arts of the occupied Palestinian territories', *Macalester International* 23/1 (2009), p. 14.

10 Oren Yiftachel, '"Ethnocracy": The politics of judaizing Israel/Palestine'. In *Across the Wall: Narratives of Israeli-Palestinian History* (eds.) Ilan Pappé, Jamil Hilal (London: I.B. Tauris, 2010), p. 290.

11 Pierre Bourdieu, 'Social space and symbolic power', *Sociological Theory* 7/1 (1989), pp. 14–25.

12 Sarab Abu-Rabia-Queder, 'The biopolitics of declassing Palestinian professional women in a settler- colonial context', *Current Sociology* 67/1 (2019), pp. 141–58.

158 Notes

13 Beshara Doumani, 'Palestine versus the Palestinians? The iron laws and ironies of a people denied', *Journal of Palestine Studies* 36/4 (2007), pp. 49–64, p 50.

14 Ibid., p. 50.

15 Nancy Scheper-Hughes, 'A talent for life: Reflections on human vulnerability and resilience', *Ethnos* 73/1 (2008), pp. 25–56.

Chapter 9

1 Beshara Doumani, 'Nablus taht al-ihtilal: mashahid min al-hayat al-yawmiyya' ['Nablus under occupation: Scenes from daily life'], *Majallat al-Dirasat al-Filistiniyyah* 62 (Spring 2005), pp. 153–63, p. 162.

2 Glenn Bowman, '"A country of words": conceiving the Palestinian nation from the position of exile'. In *The Making of Political Identities* (ed.) Ernesto Laclau (London: Verso, 1994), pp. 138–70 and 'The two deaths of Basem Rishmawi: Identity constructions and reconstructions in a Muslim-Christian Palestinian community', *Identities: Global Studies in Culture and Power* 8/1 (March 2001), pp. 47–81.

3 Bowman, '"A country of words"'; Benedict Anderson, *Imagined Communities: Reflections on the Origins and Spread of Nationalism* (London: Verso, 1983).

4 Bowman, '"A country of words"' and 'Constitutive violence and rhetorics of identity: A comparative study of nationalist movements in the Israeli-occupied territories and former Yugoslavia', *Social Anthropology* 11/3 (December 2003), pp. 37–58.

5 Bowman, 'Constitutive violence and rhetorics of identity', p. 46.

6 Michael Jackson, *Lifeworlds: Essays in Existential Anthropology* (Chicago: University of Chicago Press, 2012). pp. 19–31.

Index

Abu-Hannoud story 108–10, 115
Abu-Rabia-Queder, S. 128
agriculture 1, 8, 9, 13, 15, 18, 24, 32, 35,
      49, 59, 74, 76, 77, 79, 80–2, 90, 91,
      133, 136, 137
  Bustan and feeding 97–100
  foodways 101–2
  violence and diets 92–7
Ahmad, A. 37
al-Aqsa Martyrs' Brigades 24, 39, 40, 83
al-Bireh 48
Algeria 1960 (Bourdieu) 88
Al-Nasr mosque 53
AMIDEAST 86
Ankori, G. 157 n.9
antagonism 1, 5–7, 9, 29, 31, 33, 43, 51, 66,
      107, 114, 116, 132, 138, 146 n.3
Appadurai, A. 10
Aqraba 37
Arab population 18, 29, 31, 106
Arafat, Y. 21, 39, 40, 46
Area C 12, 21, 26, 34, 44, 46, 55, 57, 66–8,
      94, 100, 102, 104, 145 n.30, 147
      n.24, 155 n.7
Asad, T. 62
Askar refugee camp 13, 96, 106–8, 115
Assira Ash-Shamaleyya 11, 12, 27, 28, 40,
      42, 90, 95–6, 108, 109, 115, 137,
      143 n.31
Awarta 11–13, 35–7, 43–5, 48, 58, 59, 68,
      81, 94–5, 110–13, 134, 137, 145
      n.30, 145 n.32, 146 n.3, 150 n.12

baladi 93, 100, 153 n.7
Basel, A. 40
Bashar 34
Bayt Eba 25
Beckett, S. 111–12
Beit Furik 11, 13, 34, 37, 87, 94

Beit Iba 27, 58
Benjamin, W. 105
Bethlehem 121, 127–8
biopolitics 60, 61, 63, 128, 135
Bourdieu, P. 67, 69, 88, 113, 128
Bowman, G. 6–7, 114, 121, 138
Brynen, R. 75
Buchmann, C. 93
Burin 1, 12, 65, 66, 68, 81, 94, 96, 137
bustan 97–100

capitalism 17, 86
censorship 45, 46, 108, 113
checkpoints 1, 2, 9, 11, 25–7, 29, 58, 61,
      91, 95, 120, 123, 131, 134
CHF International 82
citizenship 4, 43, 52, 61, 126
class
  differentiation 49, 51
  divisions 14, 51, 127, 133, 135, 136
  formation 5, 14, 48–51
collective identity 2, 3, 6, 10, 15, 18, 19, 24,
      31, 35, 43, 51, 52, 56, 102–4, 106,
      107, 111, 113–17, 137, 139
colonialism 4, 6, 10, 17, 20, 69, 86, 89–90,
      108, 120, 138
colonial rule 17, 47, 51
Communist Party 20, 74, 99
community cohesion 45, 105–6
community relations 48, 56, 76–80
confinement 28–9
corruption 24, 38, 52, 79, 80, 135
Covid-19 pandemic 60, 121, 125
credit 88

dabke 106–8, 115
Darwish, M. 111
Dayan, M. 86
Deleuze, G. 63

Index

Democratic Front for the Liberation of Palestine (DFLP) 35, 40, 74
desperation 14, 126
disillusionment 42, 46, 57, 101
dis-Orientalism 126, 157 n.9
disorientation 15, 65, 68–71, 126–9, 135, 140, 157 n.9
disparity 50, 74, 89, 100, 132
Doumani, B. 5, 18, 91–2, 129, 131

East Jerusalem 21, 61, 70, 128, 140
economy
  imagined 86–9
  implications 75
  Israeli 92
  peace 74
  political 77
  symbolic 59
  tourism 125
  and trade agreements 123
education 5, 20, 25, 27–9, 32, 47, 49, 56, 77, 87, 89, 91, 95, 101, 104, 120–1
employment 18, 26, 29, 46, 51, 76, 78, 86, 87, 120
empowerment 32, 35, 39, 49, 103, 121, 157 n.9
European Union 13, 75, 88

Fanon, F. 42–3, 50–1, 107
Fatah 12, 34–7, 39, 40, 42, 46, 47, 49, 64, 82–4, 109, 134, 135
Fayyad, S. 86, 88
Feldman, A. 7
fellah 102
figs 1, 93
first intifada 7, 11, 19–21, 24, 29, 31–8, 40, 42–9, 69, 70, 74, 76, 77, 79, 91, 92, 95, 96, 107, 110, 113, 119, 132–4, 138, 146 n.9
food
  insecurity 82, 96–7, 133, 137
  production 91, 96
  security 82, 100, 137
foodways 15, 92, 96, 101–2
Foucault, M. 60–3
Fourth Geneva Convention 76
fragmentation 14
  forces of 139

geographic 52, 86
interpretations of 14–15
and isolation 59
levels of 56
physical 3, 14, 26, 91, 138
political 43, 46, 52, 57, 109, 110, 119, 134
social 3, 14, 29, 50, 55–7, 60, 63, 68, 70, 83, 89, 90, 101, 113, 114, 117, 132, 135, 136, 139

Gaza 4, 21, 25, 26, 32, 40, 45–7, 52, 53, 56, 57, 61, 63, 70, 73, 80, 83, 120, 140
Gazit, N. 61–2
gentrification 123
González, O. 157 n.9
graffiti 45, 46, 107, 110, 111, 113–14
Graham-Brown, S. 7
grassroots mobilization 20, 31, 35, 36, 47–8, 56, 77, 79, 104, 111, 133, 134

Habash, G. 45, 134
Halper, J. 88
Hamas 24, 25, 37, 39, 40, 45–7, 63, 64, 82–4, 109, 110, 134
Hammami, R. 26, 42, 59, 77, 78
hamula (clan) 8, 12, 19, 20, 33, 41, 57–8, 132, 134
Hanafi, S. 77, 85
Harvey, D. 86
Heiberg, M. 58
Hilal, J. 43
Hilterman, J. 20
hisbeh 100
Holy Land 119–20
home gardens 92–4, 98, 100, 102, 137, 154 n.13
Huwwara 11, 12, 25

idealization 70, 102, 114, 134
identity
  cards 4, 61
  collective 2, 3, 6, 10, 15, 18, 19, 24, 31, 35, 43, 51, 52, 56, 102–4, 106, 107, 111, 113–17, 137, 139
  cultural 32, 45, 102, 107, 113
  disorientation and 68–71
  formations of 5–8
  political 5, 14, 45–8, 51
  social 8, 50

IDF 23, 24, 27, 28
imagined worlds 10
improvement strategy 9
international
    aid 22, 26, 51, 73–6, 80–3, 85, 89, 97,
        100, 133, 136
    community 73, 75, 81, 83, 85, 112, 131,
        133, 136
    cooperation 89–90
    organizations 4, 78, 81, 84, 132, 133,
        136, 137
International Monetary Fund (IMF) 78,
    81, 86, 90
isolation 1–3, 5–12, 15, 22, 26, 28, 29, 34,
    37, 43, 46, 55, 59, 60, 62, 65, 66, 69,
    70, 81, 86, 88–91, 93, 96, 101, 102,
    105, 117, 122, 127, 131, 132, 134,
    135, 140
Israel 7, 11, 20–2, 27, 31, 32, 39, 45, 47,
    51, 56, 60–3, 66–8, 70, 74–7, 80,
    87–9, 92–4, 102, 113, 123, 128,
    133, 140
Israeli
    authorities 1, 24, 26, 66, 80, 125, 126
    domination 60, 61
    forces 24, 26, 43
    intelligence 20, 64
    law and sovereignty 128
    military 1, 4, 9, 11, 12, 20, 21, 23, 25,
        28, 35, 40, 44, 46, 63, 64, 66, 67, 70,
        82, 92, 96, 111, 125, 133, 134, 139,
        155 n.7
    occupation 3, 9, 17, 44, 56, 73, 74, 83,
        86, 90, 133, 138
    rule 51
    settlement 11, 12, 25, 96, 100, 119
    soldiers 45, 58, 106, 108, 109, 113
Israeli Committee against House
    Demolitions (ICAHD) 88

Jabal al-Nar (mountains of fire) 19
Jabal Nablus 6
Jackson, M. 115
Japanese International Cooperation
    Agency (JICA) 82
Jean-Klein, I. 32
Jerusalem 4, 5, 18, 19, 21, 27, 61, 70, 120,
    121, 128, 140
Johnson, P. 59, 65

Kanafani, G. 111, 112
Kelly, T. 142 n.15
Kennan 27
Khalidi, R. 5
kinship structures 59, 65

landscape 9, 17, 20, 49, 122–4, 126–9, 132
leadership 36, 38, 41, 44, 46, 48, 52, 68–9,
    71, 77, 86, 112, 129, 131, 133, 140
legitimacy 31, 34, 46, 57, 108, 112, 113,
    128
liberation 31, 33, 37, 41, 47, 50, 89
limestone 11, 124, 125
loans 74, 76, 86–8, 90, 101, 133, 136

mandate period 5, 7, 17, 18, 48, 51, 61, 93,
    99, 107
middle-class 5, 48, 88, 136
mobilization
    grassroots 20, 31, 35, 47, 56, 104, 111,
        134
    of kinship networks 65
    mass 32, 35, 45, 56, 57, 70, 77, 104
    nationalist 49, 138
    political 7, 22, 49, 59, 79, 107, 114, 132,
        133, 139
    popular 20, 33, 134
Mt Ebal 12, 15, 22, 24, 28, 108
Mt Jerzim 22–4
Muallem, N. 48
mukhtar 112
musha'a tenure 19

Nablus 3, 7, 9–15, 18, 19, 27–9, 40
    bustan 97–100
    landscape 122–3
    neighbourhoods 93
    PA 63–4
    population 24, 67, 97, 98
    second intifada 22–5
    worlds in 10–14
Nablus-area communities 3, 57, 91, 96,
    135, 136, 138
Nablus-Ramallah road 11
Nakba 5, 7, 49, 51, 107, 157 n.9
Nassar, H. K. 106
Nassar, N. 5
national consciousness 6, 37, 42, 50, 56
national identity 5, 31, 59, 132

162 *Index*

nationalist discourse 17, 47, 114, 138
neoliberalism 73, 75, 77, 78, 81, 83, 85, 86, 88, 90
non-governmental organizations (NGOs) 36, 48, 49, 73, 74, 76–82, 85, 89, 90, 122, 133, 136
non-recognition 6, 61, 128, 129

occupied territories 1, 4, 6, 31, 45, 46, 51, 62, 78, 80, 107, 113, 133
Old City of Nablus 22–4, 53, 63–4, 85, 93, 97–100, 121–5, 137
olives 6, 11, 12, 20, 22, 66, 93, 94, 99, 102, 108, 120, 124
Orientalism 121–2
Oslo 2 21
Oslo Accords 2, 8, 21, 25, 28, 39, 52, 75–7, 86, 119, 120, 131, 132, 134, 136, 139, 155 n.7
Oslo process 24, 46, 47, 52, 56, 78, 92, 133
Ottoman 5, 7, 9, 12, 17–19, 48, 51
Ovensen, G. 58

Palestinian
    ability of 91
    autonomy 21, 29
    citizenship 52, 61
    community 1–3, 5, 6, 9, 10, 15, 24, 28, 31, 33, 35, 43, 48–50, 59, 60, 70, 73, 86, 92, 102, 111, 116, 120, 128, 133, 137, 138
    culture 47, 58, 102, 107
    intifada 56, 104
    labour 22, 92
    lives 61, 70
    NGOs 77–80, 84, 136
    panopticon 62–4
    people 3, 18, 24, 28, 29, 31, 34, 37, 43, 63, 69, 73, 113, 138, 139
    population 6, 7, 26, 28, 29, 50–2, 60, 62–4, 68, 73, 75–7, 80, 82, 86, 89, 96, 131, 135–7
    society 7, 15, 21, 32, 33, 42, 43, 49, 50, 52, 55–8, 65, 68–71, 73, 77, 79, 83, 85, 89, 90, 114, 117, 131–4, 137–9
    theatre and artwork 110
    traffic 25, 79
    villages 10, 19, 28, 45, 68, 74, 86, 93, 96, 102, 104, 107, 112, 114, 139

Palestinian Authority (PA) 3, 4, 8, 12, 14, 24–7, 34–6, 42, 46–52, 56, 57, 59–64, 74–7, 124, 133
    establishment 21, 49
    and NGOs 77, 78, 90
    payments 87
    security forces and police 64, 76
    surveillance under 39–46
    West Bank and Hamas 46–8, 84
Palestinian Communist Party (PCP) 35, 99
Palestinian-Israeli 157 n.8
Palestinian National Fund 36
Palestinian national identity 31, 59
Palestinian People's Party (PPP) 35
Palestinian Red Crescent 22, 98, 99
paranoia 43, 62–4, 67–8, 132, 135, 139
peace building 75
Peacock, J. 116
Peteet, J. 21
physical fragmentation 3, 14, 26, 91, 138
PLO 35, 39, 41, 43, 49, 74, 94, 111, 133
political
    fragmentation 43, 46, 52, 57, 109, 110, 119, 134
    identity 5, 14, 45–8, 51
    leadership 46, 52
    mobilization 7, 22, 49, 59, 79, 107, 114, 132, 133, 139
    movements 14, 20, 31–40, 42, 45, 46, 52, 57–9, 62, 65, 85, 91, 111, 122, 134, 135
    parties 31, 32, 34–40, 42, 44, 45, 52, 53, 57, 70, 71, 77, 79, 134, 136, 139, 140
    theatre 110–13
    violence 116
Popular Front for the Liberation of Palestine (PFLP) 12, 20, 35, 36, 39, 40, 42, 44, 45, 48, 74, 95, 111, 113, 134, 146 n.3, 150 n.12
poverty 9, 12, 14, 25, 26, 62, 67, 69, 74, 82, 89, 94–6, 101, 126, 133, 145 n.30
power
    ambiguities of 83–6
    relations 3, 18, 34, 40, 63, 75, 78, 85, 131, 133
    state 61–2

al-Qassam, Shaykh 'Iz al-Din 111

Index

Rabba, M. 71
Rabin, Y. 21
radical individualism 67
Ramallah 48–50, 58, 66, 87, 110, 113
resilience 26–8, 65, 73, 85, 91, 93, 96, 102, 120, 129
resistance 6, 11, 24, 31–3, 35, 36, 38, 40, 43–7, 51, 56, 60, 64, 66, 67, 69, 78, 83, 97, 104, 107, 111, 113, 122, 140
resistance activity 32, 33
returnees 49
rural areas 8, 17, 19, 25–6, 32, 43, 50, 52, 79, 81, 89, 91, 92, 120, 133, 146 n.3

Said, E. 121–2
Scheper-Hughes, N. 129
Sebastia 13, 123–6
Second Aliyah 18
second intifada 1–3, 6–9, 11–14, 20, 22–9, 31, 38–41, 43–6, 52, 56, 57, 60, 62–5, 67, 69, 70, 73, 75, 83–5, 91–9, 101, 104–6, 111, 112, 114, 117, 120, 122, 125, 127, 131–5, 137, 138, 140
sense, making 104, 105, 113–17
Shomron National Park 125
Slyomovics, S. 33
social
    expressions 113–14
    fragmentation 3, 14, 29, 50, 55–7, 60, 63, 68, 70, 83, 89, 90, 101, 113, 114, 117, 132, 135, 136, 139
    identity 8, 50
    organization 14, 33, 42, 43, 46, 47, 56, 57, 65, 70, 104, 116, 134, 135, 139
    structures 8, 15, 18–20, 22, 34, 43, 48, 56, 57–62, 65, 73, 75, 89, 133
solidarity 7, 18, 22, 29, 31, 42–4, 47, 48, 51–3, 56, 59, 69, 70, 74, 88, 92, 93, 104, 105, 110, 113, 114, 116, 120, 127, 132, 136, 138–40
sovereignty 4, 21, 51, 61, 62, 128
Soviet Union 36, 74, 76
state power 61–2
Storyteller, The (Benjamin) 105
storytelling 103, 105–8, 111, 113, 139

surveillance 2, 4, 24, 25, 39–46, 62–5, 113, 126, 132, 135, 139, 147 n.24

Tabari, L. 77, 85
Tamari, S. 7–8, 20, 26, 32, 42, 43, 47–8, 74, 92, 102
Tanzimat 19
Taraki, L. 47, 48, 57
Tariq 45, 58, 134
Tartir, A. 84, 85
Taussig, M. 69
Tawil-Souri, H. 61, 75, 79, 80
tiger skin 28
Toriq 111–13
tourism 13, 119, 120, 125, 127
trauma 6, 26, 83, 101, 103, 107, 115, 116, 122

uncertainty 4, 11, 15, 28, 59, 63, 65, 67–8, 76, 88, 107, 126, 135, 136, 138–40
unemployment 21, 25, 27, 87, 89, 90, 122
Unified National Leadership of the Uprising (UNLU) 32
United States 47, 48, 75, 88
United States Agency for International Development (USAID) 79–82, 88
UN Office for the Coordination of Humanitarian Affairs (OCHA) 27
Usher, G. 39, 43

violence 6, 7, 11, 12, 21, 47, 60, 65, 68, 69, 88, 92–7, 103, 114–16, 120, 128

Waiting for Godot (Beckett) 111–12
Wedeen, L. 115
Weizmann, E. 23
West Bank 1–4, 8, 9, 11–13, 17, 19–21, 25–8, 32, 36, 42, 43, 46, 48, 50–3, 57, 61, 65, 69, 70, 73, 75, 76, 82, 86, 97, 104, 119, 120, 127, 133, 139
World Bank 75, 78, 81, 90, 136
Wretched of the Earth, The (Fanon) 107–8

Yusuf, S. 18

za'tar 11, 93

Made in United States
North Haven, CT
23 April 2024